Fusion Press
a division of
Satin Publications Limited
20 Queen Anne Street
London W1M 0AY
Email: sheenadewan@compuserve.com

Cover: ©1999 Nickolai Globe
Layout: Justine Hounam
Printed and bound by The Bath Press Ltd.

©1999 Andy Gravette
ISBN: 1-901250-77-6

The Saucy Little Book

Andy Gravette

Andy Gravette – Author

With a background in journalism and the press, as well as experience as a Foreign Correspondent in Africa and the Middle East, Andy Gravette writes on a variety of subjects for numerous publishers. His work with The Sunday Times and the Economist took him to West Africa, Saudi Arabia, the Seychelles and the Caribbean, where he became fascinated with Cuba. In 1984, Fidel Castro's brother introduced him to traditional Cuban cookery, and Hemingway's boat captain, Gregorio Fuentes, taught him about Cuban cigars, tobacco, and Cuban rum! Since then, Andy has written several guidebooks to Cuba, and others to destinations from Egypt to the French Caribbean. With around 30 books published, Andy has recently written the first classic Cuban cookery book, a guide to the architectural heritage of the Caribbean, a book on Irish cookery, and another on the cuisine of Wales, all due for publication shortly. Andy also lectures to tour groups on all aspects of the Caribbean.

Conversions into Imperial and Metric Measurements

Although many cooks still use the British Imperial weights and measures, Metric is fast becoming the accepted method in the kitchen. Imperial does not convert easily into Metric, and most recipe books round the resulting figures either up or down, to the nearest unit of 25g (almost one ounce).

Solid Weights

Imperial . . . . . . Metric recommended
1oz 25g
2oz 50g
4oz 100g
8oz (1/2 lb) 225g
12oz 350g
14oz 400g
16oz (1lb) 450g
2lbs 3oz 1000g (1kg)

Liquid Measures

Imperial . . . . . . Metric recommended
1/4 pint 150ml
1/2 pint 300ml
1 pint 600ml
1 1/2pints 900ml
1 3/4 pints . . . . 1000ml (1 litre)

Spoon measures

Standard spoon measures are used throughout, and all spoonfuls are level measures except where specified.

1 tablespoon = 15ml spoon
1 teaspoon = 5ml spoon

Cup measures

These vary with the ingredient, although a general rule for the size of cup is one that contains 8 liquid ounces, 1/2 pint, or 300ml of liquid.

1 cup flour = 4oz (100g)
1 cup uncooked rice = 6oz (150g)
1 cup sugar = 8oz (200g)

Oven temperatures

Both moderate and hot ovens are suggested in the recipes, and a moderately hot oven should be 160-180°C, 325-350°F, or gas mark 3-4. A hot oven should be between 220-230°C, 400-450°F, or gas mark 7-8.

Always wash fresh ingredients before preparation.

Medium sized eggs are used in all cases, except where stated otherwise.

Beans and pulses

With pulses and beans, the canned variety may be used, and around half the quantity of canned pulses equal the dried, soaked and cooked equivalent. Note that kidney beans contain harmful toxins and should always be fast-boiled for approximately 20 minutes to destroy the toxins.

Herbs

Dried herbs can be substituted where fresh herbs are unavailable, but half the quantity indicated is sufficient.

Chillies and Peppers

Warning: always prepare fresh chillies under running water if you are sensitive to their heat, and avoid contact with the eyes or sensitive parts of the anatomy until you have washed your hands thoroughly.

Peanuts

Warning: a number of people can have a violent reaction to the slightest hint of peanuts, or peanut oil. These reactions can be fatal in extreme cases.

Aphrodisiacs

Warning: some aphrodisiacs can have harmful effects and should be avoided, especially by those with medical problems. Doctors should always be consulted when considering taking any herbal medicine or aphrodisiac preparation. Drugs and similar substances should be avoided by pregnant women and young children. Absinthe, alcohol, kava kava, mandrake, nux vomica, Spanish fly and wormwood are all poisons.

sauce n. & v.

   –n.
1. Any of various liquid or semi-solid preparations taken as a relish with food; the liquid constituent of a dish (mint sauce; tomato sauce; chicken in a lemon sauce).
2. Something adding piquancy or excitement.
3. colloq. impudence, impertinence, cheek.
4. US stewed fruit etc. eaten as dessert or used as a garnish.

–v.tr.
1. colloq. be impudent to; cheek.
2. archaic a season with sauce or condiments. b add excitement to.

Etymology ME f. OF ult. f. L salsus f. salere sals – to salt f. sal salt

Oxford English Dictionary

The Saucy Little Book

x

Contents

Aphrodisia in the Kitchen

"La mejor salsa del mundo es el hambre." (*The best sauce in the world is hunger.*)
Miguel de Cervantes, author of 'Don Quixote' (1547-1616)

Salt was known as the 'staff of life' by the ancients from Africa through to Athens, and is the most fundamental and basic seasoning. It was known by the Romans as 'salsus', or 'salsa', which is where the words 'sauce' and 'saucy' come from. It is also much easier to say than 'condimentum', the Latin word for sauce! Sauces are generally liquids that are added to a savoury or sweet dish, to enhance its flavour, complement the food, or add relish to the preparation. Sauces can be marinades, concocted to slowly impart a particular flavour to food, either before it is cooked, or during cooking. Sauces can also be used as side dishes, as dips, or as a relish.

The word 'sauce' can describe also something risqué, rude or exotic and, in this context, it is interesting to note that many of the ingredients used in the preparation of sauces are said to have aphrodisiac properties. The various meanings of the word have changed over the years, but it can apply to clothes, hence 'a saucy little number', or to suggestive music. It was a famous rumba singer, Ignacio Pinerio, who, in 1928, first encouraged his band to "put a little sauce" into their music, and so heralded the beginning of Salsa music. No doubt he was referring to the fiery Cuban chilli sauces, which were famed for making Havana nights hot in more ways than one!

Fruits, vegetables and extracts often make up the body of sauces, salsas, chutneys and preserves, but it is the addition of a mixture of herbs and spices that give them their real character. The clever combination of common and exotic herbs and spices is the essence of the final creation, and each ingredient plays a special part in the concoction. Creating a sauce or salsa is an art of chemistry as much as cookery, as the ingredients react with each other to form a greater whole and the final result depends on precise measurement, careful combinations, and an intimate knowledge of the power of the ingredients.

The row of herb and spice containers on every kitchen shelf conceals a wealth of flavours, and aromas and is the culmination of thousands of years of research and alchemy. Apart from healing qualities of herbs and spices in the kitchen, these powders, seeds, stems, roots, leaves, barks, pods and flowers hold many more mysterious secrets than those used in the culinary art. Many of the herbs and spices used in everyday cuisine not only have some beneficial medicinal properties, they are also considered to have aphrodisiac qualities.

With so many concoctions, innuendoes, and intimations, it is hard to separate food from sex. We even use the term 'sexual appetite' to describe lust. The very act of eating can be related to sexual foreplay, as one of the most popular activities before sex is the enjoyment of an intimate meal. The warm internal feeling produced when eating, softens the mind and body towards more physical contact. How much more so can this sensation be enhanced by the addition of evocative herbal sauces, or exotic spicy salsas, to the meal?

The Language of Love

THE HISTORY OF APHRODISIA

An Introduction to Aphrodisiacs

"But a woman's words to an eager love
Should be written in wind and running water."
Caius Valerius Catullus (87-54 BC)

Aphrodisia is the study of the art of erotic stimulation; an art that also embraces scientific principles and dates back to the biblical Garden of Eden. Anything that arouses or stimulates, erotic or sexual desire, is known as an aphrodisiac. From whispered words to wafted scents, from erotic images to the tender touch, an aphrodisiac has the power to sensually excite. But the most intimate aphrodisiacs are undoubtedly those that are consumed by mouth.

From the beginning of time, all manner of foods and drinks were claimed to be imbued with sexually exciting properties. Just as primitive man discovered that the use of certain barks and herbs could be used as contraceptives, so the earliest pagans celebrated fertility with the use of natural aphrodisiacs. Ancient civilisations, with a lesser need for contraception, enthusiastically pursued the latter. The more scarce and valued the aphrodisiac, the more endowed it was with powers to sensually excite.

The apple is one of the earliest examples of a food being presented as love's icon. The apple was one of man's first foods, and it represented fertility. In Classical times, and earlier, the apple was the accepted symbol of sexual seduction. To the ancients, it embodied the ultimate aphrodisiac. But, by Medieval times, aphrodisiacs were regarded as sinful and 'forbidden fruit'. Therefore, when translators of the Bible came across the object that Eve proffered to Adam, they opted for the image of an apple. Later in the Book of Genesis, Leah seduces Jacob with dudaim, translated variously as mandrake, or in the Song of Solomon, as 'apple'.

Dudaim derives its name from 'dudim', a word for the pleasures of love, and the red-orange fruit of the mandrake is variously known as Satan's apple, or Love apple. The aubergine, or eggplant, is also known as the Apple of Love, thought to be a reference to the velvety semblance of its inside lobes to those of the labia.

Later, in Roman mythology, the goddess Juno gives golden apples from the Garden of Hesperides to her husband, Jupiter, as a symbol of love. With the arrival of the tomato in Europe, from the mysterious lands of the Americas, this fruit took the mantle of the 'love apple' or aphrodisiac, as tomatoes blush from green to red when ripening, and its flesh resembles intimate parts of the female genitalia. In the 1640s, Cromwell's Roundheads, declared that the fruit contained a fatal poison, as they feared that the tomato contained morally corrupting powers. Sweet potatoes, also imported at great expense from the Americas in the 16th century, were accredited with aphrodisiac qualities. In 1618, John Fletcher wrote the play 'The Loyal Subject', in which a chapter implores: "Will your Lordship please to taste a fine potato? 'T'will advance your withered state, fill your honour with noble itches."

References to love potions, philtres and aphrodisiacs are liberally sprinkled throughout 16th and 17th century literature. Shakespeare's works are littered with erotic innuendoes and references to foods that sexually excite or inflame. He recounts the classical tale of Medea, the sorceress, who rejuvenates her father-in-law with aphrodisiac herbs in 'The Merchant of Venice'. But it is to the Classical world that we must look for the origins of our language of love.

Classical Aphrodisia

It was the Greek Goddess of Love, Aphrodite, who lent her name to the word 'aphrodisia'. Born in the foam at the sea's edge, the beautiful Aphrodite became the wife of Hephaestos, and mother of Eros, the Greek god of love, and counterpart of the Roman god, Cupid. Cupid was also known as the god Amor, from where we get the word 'amorous'. It is from Eros that we get our word 'eroticism', for sexual desire or excitement. Eros became the Greek's god of earthly, or sexual, desire and gave us the word 'erogenous', the term for the rise in sexual desire, and that for particularly erotic zones of the body, which can be stimulated to arouse and increase sexual feelings. From this, we also get the words 'erotology', the study and description of love-making, or sexual activity, and 'erotomania', the word used to describe a pre-occupation with sexual passion, and an excessive erotic desire, practised by the erotomaniac.

The goddess Aphrodite wore a girdle known as the Cestus, which was embroidered with so many erotic symbols that nobody, not even Zeus, the father of the gods, could resist its seductive powers. So sexually precocious was the goddess, that she was often called Aphrodite Porne, or Aphrodite the Whore, which is incidentally the etymology of pornography. Another myth that ascribes aphrodisiac qualities to the apple is that of Paris and Aphrodite – the god Paris awarded a golden apple to Aphrodite as a token of her status as the Queen of Beauty. That Aphrodite was born of the sea is no coincidence, as many different types of seafood have long been known to contain aphrodisiac qualities. At the Greek celebrations of the festival of Aphrodisia, the temple's sorceresses, priestesses and whores, known as the Hetairae, would provide the revellers with a variety of aphrodisiac potions and philtres.

The ancient witches of Thessaly, in northern Greece, were noted for the unusual ingredients of some of their love potions, one of which was Satyrion, named for the Satyrs, or lustful woodland deities who followed the god Dionysus, or Bacchus. The 1st century Roman satirist, Petronius, in his 'Satyricon', refers to satyrion as an aphrodisiac, as does the Roman naturalist Pliny the Elder. This mysterious aphrodisiac, is said to be one of a number of orchids, but its true ancient origin is long since forgotten. The Satyrs were personified in the image of the lecherous god, the cloven-hoofed Pan, initially a Greek deity, who was also associated with another aphrodisiac, pine kernels. The 1st century Roman writer, Ovid, endorsed the powers of the pine kernel in his book, 'Remedia Amores'.

One of Greece's legendary sorceresses, Circe, makes her name in mythology by administering a magical draught to Ulysses, during his Odyssey, which brings him and his companions under her enchantment. Another name for mandrake, the aphrodisiac she is thought to have used, is Circe's Plant. It was Hermes who provided the voyager with the antidote to Circe's philtre, in the form of the herb moly. Today we use the word Circean poison for a potion that is magically, and fatally, infatuating. Another favourite Greek aphrodisiac was the carrot, which they called philon, their word for 'loving', and whose phallic shape and orange blush automatically stimulates the imagination.

The Roman goddess of love, Venus, gave us the word venereal, relating to sexual desire or intercourse, from the Latin veneris, or sexual love. Venus also lent her name to a powerful aphrodisiac, vervein, which the Roman's called the 'Luck of Venus', or Veneris vena. So potent were the plant's aphrodisiac qualities, that the Roman Emperor, Nero, had his wining and dining chambers showered with vervein and other scented flowers, pouring from sliding ivory panels set in the ceilings, to create an erotic atmosphere. The Romans also named another aphrodisiac, wormwood (Artemisia absinthium), after the Greek goddess of the moon, Artemis, and the hunter goddess of the Romans, Diana.

Fifty years before Nero's suicide, the poet Ovid wrote in his 'Remedia Amores', or Love Remedies, of simple herbs and seeds which had aphrodisiac properties, and also penned the detrimental effects of more exotic love potions, which were known to drive men mad, or sometimes had fatal consequences. The Emperor, Caligula, could well have heeded the sage's advice, as the aphrodisiacs administered by his wife turned him into a lunatic, proclaiming himself a god, declaring that his horse was a Consul, and having his banquet guests hurled into the sea!

Forty years after Caligula was assassinated, the Emperor Vespasian introduced penalties of fines, exile or even death, to those who administered aphrodisiacs which resulted in fatalities. Surpassing the Greeks in their search for erotic stimuli, and even more exotic aphrodisiacs, the Romans were noted for their orgiastic festivals, associated with Venus and the god of wine, Bacchus, from which we get our word 'Bacchanalia', or drunken revelry. During these celebrations, wine and beer flowed in rivers and many aphrodisiacs were consumed. These included spears of asparagus, carrots carved as phallus, cakes made with anise, onions, garlic, beans, pine kernels, nettles, white truffles, morels, vervein, rocket, savory, fennel, figs and all manner of exotic meats and fish, including peacock's brains, lark's tongues, oysters and sturgeon's roe. Not only were their feasts obscenely extravagant and excessive but, as a prelude to the climactic orgy which followed, musical interludes, erotic poetry readings and extravaganzas of the most lewd and often gory nature entertained the diners. Everything was designed to heighten the sexual prowess of the revellers. The Romans even had a muse of erotic poetry, Erato, 'the Lovely', depicted with a seductive lyre in her left hand.

The gods, Bacchus and Venus had a son named Priapus, a deity that personified the power of generation and who was depicted in phallic statues, which the Romans surrounded with the sacred herb rocket. Rocket was well known for its aphrodisiac qualities in ancient times, as the Roman poet, Martial, wrote in his lewd 'Epigrammata'. Both Ovid and Pliny endorsed his findings.

It was around 50 years after the death of Vespasian that a Roman fable arose around the aphrodisiac known as mandrake. A demon was said to inhabit the plant's curiously shaped roots, whose shriek at being pulled from the ground would scare the culprit to death. Several antidotes to the demon's revenge were proposed. One such, was drawing three rings around the plant with a willow wand, and tying a black thread from the plant to the collar of a white dog, thus ensuring that the harvester would be impervious to the demon's spell.

The Evolution of Aphrodisia

The ancient cultures of the Far East, India, Egypt and Arabia all sought the ultimate sexual stimulant, and it was this quest that really put aphrodisiacs on the map. In the Far East, the Indians and Chinese had evolved sects and religions around the art of sexual invigoration. The ancient Egyptians and Arabs had created stimulating unguents and exotic potions, both for the mind and body, and the Greeks and Romans revelled in lasciviousness, deifying and glorifying the sexual act. Inevitably, the debauched Romans resorted to invoking their gods to participate in their sexual abandons, which included every excess and this eventually contributed to the downfall of their empires.

An immense amount of literature written on aphrodisiacs did not survive – much was destroyed when Alexandria's great library burned and much knowledge ended up on the pyres of a succession of witch hunts. By the onset of the Dark Ages, the ancients had tested the aphrodisiac properties of just about every substance and natural living thing available. But it was only after Christopher Columbus opened up the exotic Americas, that a vast new cornucopia of aphrodisiacs flooded into the Old World. However, the puritanical nature of the Christian religion suppressed the use of aphrodisiacs, suggesting that excessive sexual indulgences detracted from leading a 'pure' life, and limited their converts' contribution to the holy church.

The use of herbs and potions, even in medicinal preparations, were thought to be pagan in origin, and therefore could never be endorsed by the church, who persecuted the dispensers of both remedies and aphrodisiacs alike. Therefore, much of the knowledge of the ancients and that of the alchemists and herbal 'sorcerers' of old has disappeared. Today, however, herbal medicine and the study of aphrodisiacs are undergoing a renaissance.

The re-birth of an interest in the aphrodisiacs of past times, and the discovery of exotic properties in newly found plants and herbs, has rejuvenated the science and art of aphrodisia. Even the pharmaceutical industry has made breakthroughs, most notably with the recent commercial release of a chemical product in the form of blue pills known as Viagra.

There are at least five divisions of the science and art of aphrodisia.
These include:

1) Foods and drinks which excite through the palate and internally
2) Fragrant scents and aromas which stimulate through the olfactory nerves
3) Beauty in form and colour which arouse the erotic through the eyes
4) Physical sensations which arouse through touch
5) Pleasing music, words and sounds which are aurally evocative

The Erotic Kitchen

"Fetch me that flower; the herb I show'd thee once;
The juice of it on sleeping eyelids laid
Will make man or woman madly dote
Upon the next live creature that it sees."
William Shakespeare (1564-1616) in 'A Midsummer Night's Dream'

The kitchen and sex have long been associated, as sexual activity is not just the reserve of the bedroom. Food is the stuff of life, and sex is the source of life, so it is no coincidence that the kitchen is a popular scenario for sex, and the stove is often a preface to silky sheets. The aromas of cooking, the warmth of the kitchen and a well-stocked larder all contribute to incline the senses towards amorous activity. In the past, country cottages often comprised of just one room, where cooking was done over the single fire, and the marital bed was located next to the hearth. As such, the relationship between sex and the kitchen was even closer.

The kitchen is also crammed with images of a sexual nature. The butt of music-hall jokes, these include all manner of fruits and vegetables, from asparagus, avocado, bananas and celery, to cherries, cucumbers, strawberries and tomatoes. Apart from these obvious references to sexual organs, the kitchen contains many more subtle sexy ingredients, a hundred or so of which promise to put a little more than a bit of spice in your life! In the following chapters, these spices, herbs, fruits and vegetables and their uses and aphrodisiac qualities are described in more detail.

If you know where to look, the average kitchen is overflowing with aphrodisiacs. Even if you live on takeaways, most people consume at least one culinary aphrodisiac every day. Aphrodisiacs may induce sexual interest purely through their odour or aroma. Other foodstuffs may stimulate through their shape, texture or chemical composition. Although the preparation of the dish is very important and may contribute to heightening the senses, often it is the ingredients cunningly concealed in a sauce or marinade that actively promotes arousal, making the dish 'fit to be set before a Queen'. After all, we know the effect of a hot chilli sauce! Is it just the heat of the sun, which is said to make the Latin races romantically volatile, or is it that their food is prepared with fiery sauces?

Aphrodisiacs and Sauces

Named after the Greek goddess of love, Aphrodite, sexual stimulants or aphrodisiacs have fascinated men and women through the ages. Every civilisation and era have left us references outlining the use of aphrodisiac mixtures; from the ancient Greeks, who favoured onions, eggs, carrots, honey and various seafood, to the aphrodisiac sauces of Renaissance France, and onto Viagra of modern times. The widespread use of aphrodisiacs even disturbed politicians through the ages. Vespasian, the Roman Emperor, decreed exile and sometimes execution of those administering aphrodisiacs.

Writers as far-flung as the French Marquis de Sade, with his '120 Days of Sodom', the Arab, Sheikh Nefzawi, with 'The Perfumed Garden for the Soul's Delectation', and the Indian, Vatsyana, with 'Kama Sutra', all detailed the preparation and uses of aphrodisiac potions. The Orient has long been a hot-bed of aphrodisiac pedlars, with Indian and Chinese potions derived from the most diverse animal sources, including rhino horn and various intimate parts of bears and tigers. The range of aphrodisiac potions is limitless, and aphrodisiac powers were once attributed to such unlikely candidates as potatoes, or toad's hearts! More universally accepted to contain aphrodisiac qualities, are such natural products as ginseng root, truffles, chocolate, and the remains of crushed beetles, known as 'Spanish Fly'.

Many ingredients used in sauces and marinades not only impart flavour to the preparation, but have other active properties. For thousands of years, man has recognised the importance of some foods as aphrodisiacs, and used these to boost their sexual desire and improve love-making. Some aphrodisiac fruits, vegetables, nuts, herbs and spices were eaten raw, whilst others were used in potions, powders or pastes. The more aromatic aphrodisiacs formed the basis of perfumes, to arouse sexual interest, and others were made into poultices or creams and applied to relevant organs.

A number of exotic ingredients of preparations thought to have aphrodisiac powers crop up regularly throughout history. Seafood such as lobster, sturgeon, caviar, oysters, sea urchins, certain seaweeds and sea cucumbers (probably selected because of their shape) all appear in aphrodisiac recipes from ancient Greece to the modern day. They are associated with Venus, the goddess of the sea, and their phosphorous, and iodine, content is an essential aphrodisiac ingredient.

There are around a hundred plants that are used in numerous culinary sauce preparations. In the following chapters, we will see that many sauce ingredients have aphrodisiac and medicinal properties. The uses of these sauce ingredients are explained and described, and should produce a smile, if not more, when enjoying sauces made from these ingredients. We also look at how seeds, stems, leaves, plants, fruits and roots are used in sexual stimulation.

Saucy Evolution

Throughout history, a variety of sauces have evolved, depending on the ingredients available. Today, there are several hundred herbs, spices, fruits and vegetables used in the making of sauces, salsas, dips, marinades and relishes. So varied and easily available are sauces of every kind, that few diners will think of sitting down to a meal which has not been prepared with a sauce, or not adding sauce to the dish on the table. From the 'high' sauces of French cuisine, to the 'lowly' tomato sauce, and from the bland to the piquant, many sauces are regional in origin, bringing the zest of the Caribbean or the zing of Chinese cookery to the dining tables of the world.

The preference of Latin countries like South and Central America for bitingly hot sauces, had remained a mystery to much of the outside world until the early days of the 20th century. Previously, the Victorian era was one of bland, thick, white or brown sauces, which often smothered the food it was intended to enhance. Gradually, with the ease of travel to the European colonies of Africa and Asia, exotic spices and herbs found their way back to the kitchens of 19th century Europe. The Mediterranean countries had long been trading in condiments from the East, and several nations had made their fortunes from the spice routes. However, few 19th century cooks were bold enough to place foreign foods, like Indian curries or Chinese chop sueys on the tables of Europe.

Traditional sauces, particularly those popularised by French chefs, remained stalwart ingredients on the menus of the Northern European table until a few adventurous cooks broke free of the bonds of insipid sauces. Although the Spanish had the advantage of importing herbs and spices from both the Far East and their colonies in the New World, opened up by Columbus in the 1500's, they were reluctant to experiment with these exotic ingredients for several centuries.

It was on the Mediterranean island of Ibiza that the ingredients of East and West first really came together, when a Spanish cook combined a mixture of exotic ingredients which came to be known as Garam Masala.

Today, this mixture of spices and herbs forms the basis of many Oriental dishes. Around the same time as the creation of Garam Masala, another chef on the nearby island of Menorca began producing a sauce known as 'salsa mahonesa', named after the island's capital, Mahon. Today, this universally used dressing is widely known as mayonnaise. Not generally used in cooking, it is a mixture of egg yolks, mustard, white wine vinegar, olive oil, pepper and salt, and used to enhance salads.

Towards the end of the 19th century, a number of civil servants and military personnel began returning from Europe's colonies, where they had acquired a taste for the exotic! This not only applied to their lifestyle, but also to their palates. Kedgeree, the Eastern rice and fish concoction, with its sprinkling of aromatic seasoning, became a popular breakfast dish and it was not long before returning colonials were demanding curries at their dinner tables.

All the while, in the island colonies of the West Indies, the European sugar growers steadfastly stuck to their traditional homeland fare, blissfully ignorant of the exotic dishes being prepared by their subordinates. From the 17th to the 19th century, the plantation owners, in mansions that replicated those in Europe, rigidly abided by home-cooking, importing many of the ingredients at vast expense. Even the local rum was shunned in favour of imported wine and ale, well into the 19th century.

However, in the kitchens of the West Indies, local cooks were busily creating a mysterious cuisine which came to be known as Afro-Caribbean, one of the most varied of all culinary achievements. Afro-Caribbean cookery relied on local ingredients, some brought there by enslaved Africans, and others which arrived with indentured workers from the Far East. The wide range of ingredients and recipes from three continents soon combined with those of Europe, bringing a completely new taste to the culinary world.

The Cradle of Salsa

It is hard to imagine that African, Thai or even Indian dishes were once prepared without the use of chillies or sweet peppers as well as many other exotic spices and herbs. For thousands of years, secrets of these ingredients, now commonplace in modern day cuisine, had eluded the ancients of Asia, Europe and the Mediterranean. The use of chillies, sweet peppers, peanuts, tomatoes, sunflowers and many other exotic spices and herbs in international cuisine is just 500 years old, although they were being grown in Central and South America, and the

Caribbean as far back as 5000 BC.

Half a millennium ago, the entire culinary spectrum across the world was changed by the discovery of the New World and its cornucopia of sauce ingredients. Just as it is difficult to envisage a curry without the heat of chillies, the Hungarian goulash minus a pinch of paprika or con carne with no chilli, it is not easy to consider a kitchen without potatoes, tomatoes, beans, sunflower oil, peanuts or maize.

No canned tomatoes, spicy sauces, hot curry powder, baked beans, corn flakes, popcorn, peanut butter or even fish and chips! Today, we take for granted these essential additions to our diet, especially those hot salsas, spicy sauces and piquant powders which are an integral addition to our kitchen shelves and on the dining table. So many tinned foods and bottled sauces owe their taste to the deceptively innocent-looking chilli, the shiny sweet pepper, the meaty grain of maize, the filling bean, or the juicy tomato. Just a humble tin of baked beans contains no less than four ingredients which were unknown outside southern America and the Caribbean before the Spanish sailed west – tomato pureé, corn starch, chillies and the beans themselves!

It was in the Caribbean town of Angostura, back in 1824, that one of the first commercial sauces was marketed. Angostura Bitters, an aromatic sauce used widely in all forms of cookery, soon became synonymous with the island of Trinidad, from where it was distributed world wide. Not far from Trinidad, in the north of the Caribbean, the southern states of America were acquiring a taste for the hot Mexican style of cooking. In 1868, an entrepreneur from Louisiana began to produce a fiery sauce from Mexican chillies, which he called Tabasco, after the place in Mexico. In Jamaica, a bottling plant began manufacturing another hot sauce in 1921. Known universally, it is a combination of classic ingredients: tomatoes, onions, peppers, chillies, raisins, mangoes, tamarinds, salt, pepper, spices, cane vinegar and sugar. Since then, hundreds of different sauces have been produced commercially, and whether spicy, herby or hot, most contain that distinctive of ingredients – the chilli.

In the 1830's, the English made a sauce known as ketchup, from herbs, walnuts, cucumbers and brine. It was known as ketchup from the Malaysian sauce called 'ketsiap', made with the brine of pickled fish. Henry J. Heinz opened his grocery shop in America in 1869, but it was not until 1876 that he began producing 'catsup', in gallon whiskey barrels. In 1886, he travelled from Sharpsburg, Pennsylvania, to London with five hampers of his product. The store, Fortnam and Mason bought the entire consignment, and from then on Mr Heinz's name was made. Today, Heinz bottles enough tomatoes a year to fill an Olympic swimming pool.

Other famous sauces include mushroom ketchup, made popular in 1830 by George Watkins, and the secret ingredient of many a Victorian cook. It has a taste midway between Worcestershire sauce and soy sauce. Originally, this sauce was made by packing whole mushrooms in earthenware jars, and heating them until the dark juice flowed. The jars were then boiled in the oven, and the sauce strained through muslin. Black pepper, nutmeg and mace were then added to pep up the sauce.

Worcestershire sauce was said to have been the invention of Marcus Lord Sandys, who returned from India with a formula which he asked a John Lea and William Perrin to make up for him. They found it so disgusting that the sauce was rejected, only to be re-discovered years later. It is a blend of malt, spirit vinegar, molasses, garlic, shallots, tamarind and anchovies, which is matured and filtered before other secret ingredients are added. Lea and Perrins company now make a range of sauces and marinades, and the number of commercial sauces now available runs into hundreds of thousands.

In olden times, Bechamel sauce was made with blanched onions and a bouquet garni, which was added after the sauce had been reduced and sieved. The onions and seasoning were mixed with the sauce, cooked in the oven for several hours and then strained again.

Bechamel, or Bechamelle sauce, is one of the 'three main sauces', of which the 'Prince of Gastronemers', Curnonsky, religiously shied away from using. The second of the three sauces is Espagnole sauce, a favourite in Victorian kitchens. It was originally made with a fat-free coulis, generally old chicken or partridge meat, moistened with Madeira wine and rendered down by cooking for a day or two! A more modern recipe recommends a mixture of diced ham, veal, beef and ham bones, together with diced root vegetables, such as turnips, carrots, leeks, onions and celery, flavoured with white wine, thyme, parsley and bay, all cooked together in the oven for six hours.

The third of the three sauces is Allemande sauce. This is a form of Bechamel sauce, made with stock instead of milk, and bound together with the yolks of eggs and cream.

Salt of the Earth and the Spice of Life

The Saucy Little Book' explores how the invention of culinary sauces evolved, the introduction of chillies and chilli peppers into cookery, and examples of how sauces were used to preserve meats and fish. It looks at the various exotic ingredients which are used in sauce recipes, and the range of herbs and spices used in sauces and other cookery techniques.

The 'saucy' element of food runs as a secondary theme throughout the book, looking at the aphrodisiac qualities of certain sauce ingredients, herbs and spices. Just as our basic foods are the essential 'staff of life', so sauces transform these foods into delectable delicacies which titillate the palate and make ordinary foods so much more enjoyable. Foods which are a basic necessity to life, become sensual and evocative with the use of a sauce, a feast for the eyes and the soul, as well as the taste. With the addition of sauces, the blandest food can excite the senses and inflame the passion, not just for the gourmet's delight, but for the ardour of the amorous.

However, to be reminded of the link between aphrodisiac sauces and foods, we only have to refer to the dining table and the twin condiment containers common to every home. Both the pepper and salt mills hold the secret to this book's theme. The pepper pot is used to grind fresh black peppercorns, and the salt pot to grind coarse sea salt. However, it was the Indian peppercorn which lent its name to the chilli pepper, revolutionising sauce preparations, and the word 'sauce' itself derived from the ancient word for salt. Therefore, the everyday dining table with its two grinding mills can serve as a simple reminder of the extraordinary story of sauces through the ages, and the essential part they play in cuisine around the world.

Saucy Secrets

Saucy Advice

Sauces are among the kitchen's most versatile concoctions. In early times, many sauces were created to disguise the taste of foods that were not quite fresh. Some were cooked up to make the dish more digestible, and other sauces were designed to enhance the taste of food. Many sauces complement the flavour of certain foods, and others to stimulate gastric juices or just to improve the appearance of a dish. It is tempting to make suggestions about the foods that the sauces might best suit, but this would be presumptuous in many cases, as the choice of a certain sauce to match a particular food is purely a matter of personal taste. It should never be the rule that a sweet sauce befits a sweet dish, or that a sour, bitter, spicy or chilli-hot sauce should accompany a savoury dish. On a more saucy line, it is also presumptuous to say that a sauce should be used at the table. Many sauces are indeed suited for use on the table, over the kitchen sink or in the bedroom! The preference for licking a particularly favourite sauce from a chosen flesh, preferably that of a partner, is also a matter of taste! However, to end on a cautionary note. Should the latter enjoyment of sauce appreciation appeal, be warned of the intensely irritant nature of some sauces, especially those containing chilli. In whatever way you wish to enjoy your choice of sauces, they can only add to your pleasure, whether it be at the table, in the kitchen or even out in the open air – be it at a barbecue, picnic, an outdoor meal or during an exhibitionist al fresco sexual act! Sauces are for enjoyment – so, enjoy!

"Erato why turn'st thou to magic art?
A far more subtle way I would impart!"
Ovid (43 BC-18 AD)

Just as there are thousands of magical aphrodisiacs, there are a million sauce recipes which range from the mild and bland to the fiery hot. No one book could do justice to the complete range. To propose that any one sauce is ultimately an aphrodisiac would be presumptuous, but sauces act on different people in various ways. Therefore, no claims are made for the following recipes. Likewise, no responsibility can be held for the consequences that occur from the serving of the same!

Most of these recipes can be used in a variety of ways – as marinades, dips, for barbecues, basting, roasts or just as a side dish. Some can be served hot, whilst others are best cold. Sauces, their ingredients and their application, are all down to experimentation; a rule which should also be applied to the bedroom!

DUXELLES D'AMOUR (Truffle flavoured sauce)

225g (8oz) field mushrooms, very finely chopped
5g (1/4oz) truffle, finely grated
1 medium onion, very finely chopped
2 shallots, very finely chopped
10g (1/2oz) butter
1/4 tsp salt and fresh ground black pepper, mixed
1/4 tsp nutmeg, freshly ground
1 tsp parsley, finely chopped
3 tbsp cream

Dry the mushrooms by wringing out in a cloth after washing. Fry the mushrooms, onions, shallots and parsley in butter. When the liquid has evaporated, stir in the truffle gratings. Season and spice, then stir in the cream and heat through.

SAUCE BOUDOIR (BRANDY MUSHROOM SAUCE)

675g (1 1/2lbs) button mushrooms, sliced very fine
50g (2oz) salt
2 shallots, sliced fine
1 tsp pickling spices
3 black peppercorns, crushed
2 green peppercorns, crushed
1/2 tsp ground mace
1/4 tsp allspice
juice of one lemon
1 tbsp brandy

Layer the mushrooms and salt in a bowl, set aside for 24 hours. Stir in the shallots and bake in a cool oven for 30 minutes. Puree the mushroom mixture in a blender. Add the rest of the ingredients, except the brandy, to the pureé. In a pan, slowly bring the mixture to the boil. Continue to boil for around 3 minutes, stirring. Set aside to cool, and then stir in the brandy.

STEAMY SAUCE (MUSHROOM AND TRUFFLE PUREE)

900g (2lbs) mushrooms, sliced
1/2 tsp truffles, grated
2 tbsp butter
1/4 cup margarine
2 tbsp flour
1/2 cup water
2 tsp salt
1/2 cup milk
2 tbsp lemon juice
1 tsp fresh nutmeg, grated
1/2 tsp fresh ground black pepper
1 tbsp fresh parsley, chopped

Melt the butter in a pan, add mushrooms, water and half the salt. Stir in the pepper, lemon juice and nutmeg. Boil, stirring, then simmer for 8 minutes. Strain the mixture, keeping the liquid. Pureé the mushroom mix in a blender. Melt the margarine in a pan, remove from heat. Stir in the flour, making a paste. Gradually stir in the liquid and milk, return to heat. Simmer until smooth and thick, then stir in mushroom mix. Stir in the truffles and parsely, then add rest of the salt.

CHIE SAUCE (MUSHROOM SAUCE)

110g (4oz) mushrooms, sliced fine
1/2 tsp truffles, grated
25g (1oz) butter
2 tbsp flour
175g (6oz) cream
1 cup chicken stock
1/4 tsp salt
1/4 tsp fresh ground black pepper
1/2 tsp capers, finely chopped
1 tbsp Marsala

Fry the mushrooms in the butter for 3 minutes. When brown, remove mushrooms, keeping liquid. Stir the flour into the liquid, then add the stock and stir. Cook for 2 minutes, then add capers and truffles. Season, remove from heat and stir in the cream. Finally, stir in the Marsala.

RISQUE MAYONNAISE (Mushroom, Truffle and Asparagus Mayonnaise)

225g (8oz) button mushrooms, thinly sliced
1 tsp truffles, finely sliced
450g (1lb) asparagus spears, cooked and chopped small
1 cup mayonnaise
1 tbsp chives, chopped small
6 tbsp olive oil
2 tbsp white wine vinegar
1/2 tsp salt
1/2 tsp fresh ground black pepper

Mix oil, vinegar, salt and pepper in a bowl. Beat until blended, then add mushrooms. Leave to marinade for 1/2 hour, then add asparagus. Stir in mayonnaise and chives. Sprinkle the truffles over the mayonnaise before serving.

PASSIONATE SAUCE (SPICY SAUCE)

1 onion, chopped
1 garlic clove, crushed
1 tsp fresh root ginger, finely chopped
1 celery stalk, chopped small
3 tomatoes, skinned and chopped small
25g (1oz) butter
2 tsp brown sugar
2 tbsp lemon juice
2 tbsp vinegar
2 tbsp tomato pureé
1 tbsp Worcestershire sauce
1/2 tsp dried oregano
1 bay leaf
1/4 tsp grated nutmeg
1 tsp salt

Sauté the onion and garlic in butter for 5 minutes. Add the rest of the ingredients. Bring to boil, then simmer for 40 minutes. Strain the sauce before use.

CAPRICIOUS SAUCE (ORIENTAL-STYLE SAUCE)

2 onions, finely chopped
1 tbsp butter
1 green chilli, seeded and finely chopped
2 dried red chillies, seeded and finely chopped
1 green bell pepper, seeded and finely chopped
1 tsp cumin seeds
1 tsp coriander seeds
8 cardamom pods
1 bay leaf, crumbled
5 fl oz (1/4 pint) yoghurt
3 tsp peanut oil
1/4 tsp salt and fresh ground black pepper, mixed

Crush cumin, coriander and cardamom together. Melt the butter with the oil in a pan. Cook the onion and bell pepper in butter and oil for 5 minutes. Add the spices, chillies and bay leaf. Stir, and cook for 5 minutes. Remove from heat and stir in yoghurt, adding seasoning.

EROTIC SAUCE (HOT TOMATO SAUCE)

4 tomatoes, halved and seeded
1 onion, sliced
3 Poblano chillies, cut in four lengthways
3 garlic cloves, unpeeled
1 tbsp lime juice
1/4 tsp salt and fresh ground black pepper, mixed

Place a grill tray over medium hot coals. Put the onions and garlic on the tray. Add the tomatoes, skin upwards and chillies, skin down. Turn the garlic until soft, then peel. When the chillies are browned slightly, place in a plastic bag. Turn the onions and brown slightly. Take the skins off the tomatoes when they are cooked. After 10 minutes in the closed plastic bag, skin the chillies. Place all the ingredients in blender and chop roughly.

SAUCE POMME D'AMOUR (SAUCY TOMATO GARNISH)

25g (1oz) butter
2 tomatoes, skinned and chopped
1/2 pint stock
1 tsp plain flour
1 tbsp Worcestershire sauce
1/4 tsp salt and fresh ground black pepper, mixed

Melt the butter in a pan and stir in flour. Cook gently for around 3 minutes. Remove from heat and stir in stock. Add the sauce and seasoning. Bring to the boil and add tomatoes. Simmer for around 1 minute.

RAPTUROUS SAUCE (MEXICAN-STYLE SAUCE)

2 fresh Serrano chillies, seeded and finely chopped
1 medium onion, finely chopped
1 garlic cloves, finely chopped
2 drops of Tabasco sauce
juice of 2 limes
25g (1oz) butter
1/2 tsp cumin powder
pinch of salt

Marinade onions in lime juice for 1 hour. Drain onions and save juice. Fry the onions in butter until soft. Add rest of ingredients and cook slowly for 15 minutes.

ECSTATIC SAUCE (Chilli Tomato Sauce)

6 fresh Jalapeno chillies, seeded and finely chopped
450g (1lb) tomatoes, blanched, seeded, skinned and chopped
2 medium onions, finely chopped
2 garlic cloves, finely chopped
1 tsp ground coriander
2 tbsp brown sugar
1 tbsp tomato chutney
2 tbsp tomato ketchup
1 tbsp capers, chopped small
2 fl oz (55ml) maize oil
4 tbsp water
1/2 level tsp cayenne pepper
juice of 1 lime
2 fl oz (55ml) rum
pinch of salt and pepper

Fry onions and garlic in oil until soft. Add tomatoes, salt and pepper.
Sprinkle over with sugar and bring to boil. Simmer for 5 minutes,
then add lime juice, capers and chutney. Simmer for 5 more minutes,
add rest of ingredients except rum. Bring to boil and then let cool.
Stir in the rum, then blend to a pureé.

SEVENTH HEAVEN SAUCE (FRUITY MUSHROOM SAUCE)

50g (2oz) butter
1 tsp sugar
1/2 tsp wine vinegar and Tabasco sauce, mixed
2 tbsp tomato ketchup
1 tbsp Worcestershire sauce
2 tbsp mushroom ketchup
1 tbsp fruity sauce

Melt the butter in a pan and stir in vinegar and Tabasco mix. Add all the other ingredients and mix together thoroughly.

AMATORY SAUCE (MANGO SAUCE)

2 large, ripe mangoes, peeled, stoned and diced
2 large tomatoes, seeded and finely diced
6 spring onions, finely chopped
2 garlic cloves, finely chopped
6 anchovies, finely chopped
1 Jalapeno chilli, finely chopped
juice of one lime
2 tbsp chopped coriander

Combine all ingredients in large bowl. Garnish with the coriander.

SENSUAL SAUCE (SWEET AND SOUR SAUCE)

1 onion, finely chopped
5 tbsp wine
5 tbsp Worcestershire sauce
1 tbsp tomato pureé
1 tsp mustard powder
1 garlic clove, crushed
1 tbsp soft brown sugar

Mix all ingredients together thoroughly.

RAVISHING SAUCE (PINEAPPLE SAUCE)

6 pineapple rings, quartered
4 tsp Worcestershire sauce
5 tsp honey
4 tsp tomato ketchup
1/4 tsp dried rosemary
4 tsp lemon juice
1/4 pint stock
1/4 tsp salt and fresh black pepper, mixed

Blend the pineapple rings in blender to a pureé. Heat the pureé
gently, stirring in the rest of the ingredients. When honey is melted
and ingredients mixed, remove from heat.

BACCHANALIAN SAUCE (SPICY CHILLI SAUCE)

1 small onion, finely chopped
2 shallots, finely chopped
2 red chillies, seeded and finely chopped
3 garlic cloves, finely chopped
1/2 tbsp fresh root ginger, finely chopped
2 tsp soft brown sugar
1 tsp allspice
1 tsp cinnamon powder
1 tsp fresh thyme, chopped small
1/4 tsp nutmeg, grated
1 tbsp malt vinegar
juice of 1 lime
juice of half an orange
1 tbsp vegetable oil
1/4 tsp salt and fresh ground black pepper, mixed

Mix the sauce ingredients into a stiff paste.

SEXY SAUCE (Creole-Style Sauce)

2 tbsp rum
4 tbsp vegetable oil
4 garlic cloves, minced
2 large tomatoes, skinned, seeded and chopped
1 small onion, finely sliced
2 red chillies, seeded and finely chopped
1 tsp lime juice
1/2 tsp allspice
1/4 tsp salt and black pepper, mixed

Sauté the onions in a pan in half the oil for 3 minutes. Add the garlic and chillies, and cook for 2 minutes. Add the tomatoes and lime juice, and cook stirring for 5 minutes. Add the allspice, salt and pepper and let cool. Pureé the salsa in a blender with the rum and rest of oil.

SEDUCTIVE SAUCE (Brown Tomato Sauce)

50g (2oz) butter
1/2 cup tomato pureé
1 1/2 tbsp horseradish sauce
1 1/2 tbsp gold brown sugar
1 tbsp lemon juice
1/2 tbsp Worcestershire sauce
1/2 cup white wine vinegar
1/2 tbsp salt

Mix all ingredients in a pan and simmer for 15-20 minutes. Stir whilst cooking, until mixture thickens. Serve either warm or cold.

PERFUMED THAI GARDEN SAUCE
(AROMATIC SPICY SAUCE)

2 tbsp fresh ginger root, grated
2 cloves garlic, finely chopped
175g (6oz) peanut butter
3 tbsp soy sauce
50g (2oz) sugar
1 tbsp fresh coriander, finely chopped
1/2 cup white wine vinegar
1 tbsp peanut oil
1/4 tsp cayenne pepper
1/4 tsp salt and ground black pepper, mixed
1/2 cup water

Bring the water and vinegar to boiling. Dissolve the sugar in the mixture. Remove from heat. Add all the other ingredients, except the oil. Pureé mixture in a blender until smooth. Stir in the oil thoroughly. Heat to simmering before serving.

LUSTFUL SAUCE (Caribbean-Style Sauce)

150ml (5 fl oz) pineapple juice
2 tbsp olive oil
4 tbsp soft brown sugar
1 tbsp Dijon mustard
1/2 tsp chilli powder
1/4 pint sweet white wine
1/4 tsp allspice

Mix sauce ingredients together into a smooth paste.

APHRODITE'S SAUCE (Orange Sauce)

2 tbsp tomato ketchup
3 tbsp brown sauce
2 tsp Worcestershire sauce
2 tbsp parsley, finely chopped
1 tbsp Curacao
1/4 pint orange juice
grated rind of half an orange
2 tsp lime juice
1/4 tsp salt and ground black pepper

Mix the sauce ingredients together thoroughly.

KAMA SAUCE (CURRY SAUCE)

2 green bell peppers, seeded and finely chopped
2 hot chillies, seeded and finely chopped
2 onions, chopped
1 apple, peeled, cored and chopped
1 garlic clove
2 tbsp green chutney
25g (1oz) flour
25g (1oz) butter
1/2 tsp caraway seeds
1/2 tsp cumin seeds
1 tsp cardamom seeds
1 tsp curry paste
3 tbsp curry powder
1/2 tsp salt
1/2 tsp lemon juice

Fry onion, peppers and apple in butter for 5 minutes. Add curry powder and chillies, and cook for 3 minutes, stirring. Stir in the flour. Mix the cardamom, cumin, caraway and garlic together. Stir into mixture. Stir in the curry paste and salt and add stock. Bring to boil, covering and simmering for 20 minutes. Stir in chutney and lemon juice. Simmer the sauce for 15 minutes, stirring occasionally.

EROS' SAUCE (Tamarind Sauce)

225g (1/2lb) fresh or preserved tamarind
2 tsp fresh root ginger, finely chopped
2 tbsp dark treacle
1 tsp chilli powder
1 tsp salt
570ml (1 pint) boiling water

Pour boiling water over the tamarind, allow to cool. Push the tamarind pulp through a sieve with a wooden spoon. Discard black tamarind seeds. Stir pulp, water and rest of ingredients together. Simmer mixture gently for 20 minutes.

VENUS' SAUCE (LIMEY SAUCE)

1 large onion, finely chopped
1 garlic clove, finely chopped
2 tomatoes, peeled and chopped
2 tbsp soy sauce
1/4 tsp chilli powder
1/2 tsp fresh ground black pepper
1 tsp maize oil
juice of three limes

Sauté garlic and onion in oil. When golden, add tomatoes and simmer until soft. Stir in soy sauce, and mix until smooth. Add lime juice, chilli powder and pepper, and bring to boil.

ANTICIPATION SAUCE (CREAMY MUSTARD SAUCE)

3 tsp mustard powder
1 tsp sesame seeds, toasted
2 tbsp soy sauce
1 small garlic clove, crushed
2 tbsp double cream
1 tbsp hot water

Mix mustard with the water into a paste. Add sesame seeds, soy sauce and garlic. Blend into a paste, then add cream. Stir and then serve.

ROMANCING SAUCE (ROSEMARY SAUCE)

2 shallots, finely sliced
1 tbsp fresh rosemary, finely chopped
75g (3oz) butter
1/2 cup chicken stock
3 tbsp dry white wine
3 tbsp double cream
1/4 tsp salt and fresh black pepper mixed

Sweat shallots in butter for 3 minutes. Add wine and rosemary, cooking for 4 minutes. Add stock, stirring and reduce by half. Add cream and seasoning, stir and boil for 3 minutes. Strain through sieve, return to heat, serving hot.

AROUSAL SAUCE (Pumpkin Seed Sauce)

50g (2oz) pumpkin seeds, shelled
1 small onion, finely chopped
1 clove garlic, crushed
1 Poblano chilli, seeded and finely chopped
1 slice white bread, cut into small dices
3 cups of thick chicken stock
4 tbsp single cream
2 tbsp maize oil
1/4 tsp salt

In oil, cook seeds, onion, garlic and bread pieces. When bread is golden in colour, add chilli. Cook for 1 more minute, then whisk in blender until smooth. Stir stock and cream into paste, then add salt. Return to heat and reduce by one quarter. Serve hot.

DELECTABLE SAUCE (BUTTERED SAFFRON SAUCE)

> 2 tbsp shallots, finely chopped
> 110g (4oz) butter
> 1 tbsp white wine vinegar
> 2 tbsp dry white wine
> 2 tbsp double cream
> 1/4 tsp saffron (broken threads or powder)
> 1/4 tsp salt, white pepper and nutmeg, mixed

Simmer shallots, vinegar, wine and saffron together for 2 minutes. Stir in cream and simmer again for 3 minutes. Season with salt, pepper and allspice mix. Reduce heat and stir in butter, a little at a time. Do not let sauce get too hot, then remove from heat. Whisk quickly and serve hot.

JERK SAUCE (JAMAICAN SALSA)

1 small onion, chopped
1 small green pepper, seeded
1/2 tbsp olive oil
1 tsp orange juice
1 tsp lime juice
1/4 tsp garlic powder
1/4 tsp cinnamon and allspice, mixed
1/4 tsp cayenne pepper
2 tsp sugar
1/2 tsp fresh thyme and sage, finely chopped
1 tsp salt and black pepper, mixed
1 tbsp dark soy sauce
1/4 tsp nutmeg
3 tsp white wine vinegar

Blend all ingredients together and use in barbecue.

Some Like it Hot

"Woe to the cook whose sauces have no sting!"
Early English proverb

Peppers and Chillies – The Plant and the Fruit

There are two main varieties of an American native bush which produces a range of fruit, or seed pods – from fiery hot chillies down to the sweet, mild capsicum. Both the chilli and the sweet pepper are of the genus Capsicum. The chilli plant (Capsicum frutescens) is of the same family as the capsicum, or sweet pepper plant (Capsicum annum), and both are native to the Americas. South American chillies, like the Aji and the Brazilian Malagueta, belong to the species Baccatum, and the Anaheim and Habanero chillies belong to the Chinese species.

Most chillies and peppers are easily propagated, given the right temperature, although seeds of the Habanero chilli have been genetically modified by commercial growers, to prevent inroads into their lucrative market. Chillies are grown in the tropics from sea level up to 2000m, and both chillies and peppers will grow in temperate climates in the warmer parts of the year. Grown annually, green chillies are picked after three months although some, like the Cayenne chilli, are left to ripen. The Sweet, Capsicum, Bullnose, Pimento, Paprika or Bell pepper plant, of which there are around 30 varieties, grows to only half the height of the chilli plant, which can reach 2 metres in height.

Both chillies and peppers belong to the Solanaceae family, which includes the tomato, potato and nightshade plants. Chillies generally range from yellow and orange to green and red, and peppers can also be white or purple. Generally, the annum varieties of peppers are annual plants, whilst others are perennial. There are now more than 1600 varieties of chilli and cap-sicum grown worldwide. Capsicums are among the widest cultivated spice crops in the world. Harvesting of chillies can continue for around three months. The fruits of these plants, the chillies or sweet bell peppers are shiny and can be red, green, brown, purple or yellow when ripe.

The capsicum is used both unripe when green, or ripe when they are red, yellow, purple or white. Some chillies are so hot that they can burn the hands of the pickers. Both chillies and peppers have little food value. Peppers contain around 38 calories per 100 grams. Chillies have little aroma, but range greatly in pungency, shape and colour. They are usually used fresh but are often dried when their surface wrinkles, and can be smoked or pickled.

Today, chillies and capsicum peppers are integral ingredients in international cuisine. Sweet peppers have various names depending on the region. In the Caribbean, they are known generally as Capsicum; in the French islands they are called Poivron, or Piment doux; Pimiento is the Spanish for pepper, which is why some peppers are known as pimento, not to be confused with allspice, which is also known as pimiento, and in some places the sweet pepper is known as the Bullnose. Although the capsicum variety are called peppers, they bear no relation except in their pungency to black and white pepper, which is the ground seeds, or peppercorns of the Indian pepper plant, or vine (Piper nigrum).

There are several ways of spelling chilli. Chile is the American way of spelling chilli, and the Spanish name for the chilli is also 'chile', known as 'aji' in the Hispanic Caribbean. Today, as chillies are grown outside their native New World, some are given names that relate to their commercial origin, like Thai, Kenyan or Indian chillies. Capsicum means 'little case' in Latin, named as such because both chillies and sweet peppers are hollow and contain a fleshy core, surrounded by many tiny seeds. The white seeds of both chillies and capsicums, and their veins, are usually discarded in cookeryas they can be fiery hot.

The skin of both the pepper and the chilli is tough and thin, and pepper flesh is generally thicker than that of chillies. The larger capsicum peppers have a faint, fresh smell and a slightly sweet, mild taste with just a hint of heat. Most importantly, the chilli is the main ingredient in the mix of herbs and spices used in meat preservation, essential in any hot climate. This is because the chilli contains an antibacterial agent, and both chillies and sweet peppers are rich in the Vitamins A and C.

Because of the effects of capaicin, the active ingredient in chillies, they also have many medicinal uses, and liniments and plasters for lumbago, muscle strain and neuralgia are made with chillies. In the early 1500's, Europeans quickly discovered the curative properties of the chilli. They produced cayenne from finely ground chillies, with which poultices were made to treat muscular aches and pains, and cure circulatory disorders. They also used peppers in cases of kidney or stomach ailments. Today, many Caribbean societies still prepare chillies as a medicine for colds and bronchitis. Chilli concoctions are also prepared for the treatment of unbroken chilblains and medicinally as a stimulant, and aid, to digestion and to produce warmth.

As soon as the word 'chilli' is mentioned, the 'hot' words come to mind; fiery, burning, heat, scorching, glowing, volcanic, explosive. Everyone remembers their first encounter with hot chillies – in a sauce, powder or on their own. The association is generally with the burn of the chilli, which is curiously almost a comfortable pain, but can be extreme enough to cause a temporarily unbearable pain. The essential oil in chillies, capsaicin, increases the circulation of the blood on contact, and is responsible for the 'burning' sensation that eating chillies can cause.

Chillies are used in cookery initially for their flavour, secondly for their heat and thirdly for their colour. It is capsaicin that gives the fruit its pungency. Capsaicin is also found in the seeds, skin and veins. It is this ingredient that releases endorphins, or natural opiates. When endorphins are present in the human body, a sense of well-being is experienced and it also blocks out pain. The tear ducts automatically fill the eyes with water, the skin perspires abnormally and the nose streams. Chillies can burn the eyes and skin, and even their seeds and internal membranes, or veins, are hot. Wash hands and knives thoroughly immediately after handling chillies. Some people prefer to wear gloves whilst preparing chillies. If burned whilst eating chillies, do not drink as this exacerbates the burning sensation. Instead, eat bread, plain rice, beans or dairy produce such as cheese or yoghurt. Being burned by a chilli does the opposite of putting the eater off enjoying chillies again – rather, it seems to encourage more indulgence!

Capsaicin is measured in scientific units called Scovilles, literally the Richter scale of the vegetable world. It was in 1902 that the pharmacologist Wilbur Scoville mixed ground chillies with alcohol and water, inventing a scale based on how much each mixture needed to be diluted before heat was detected. The Scoville scale ranges from the mildest, the bell pepper classified as '0', to the hottest, the Habanero, which is estimated at a staggering '300,000'! However, for ease, most cooks rate the capsaicin content of chillies in units from 0-100.

Probably the most rampant and least discreet of all aphrodisiacs, chillies are used in culinary concoctions from salads to sauces, and from soups to stews. Chillies contain Vitamin C, which produces adrenalin and other hormones, important in sexual stimulation. Capsaicin releases endorphins, natural aphrodisiacs, which impart a feeling of well-being. However, it is not recommended that chillies are used in any lotion or love potion designed to be applied to sensitive areas!

Cooking with Chillies and Peppers

Although many chillies are used in sauces, which are then added to the meal during cooking, there are three distinct methods of cooking with chillies whereby the heat of a dish can be controlled. To exclude the hotness of the chillies but retain their flavour, cook with whole chillies and discard them after cooking. To add a moderate heat, halve the chillies, removing the pith, veins and seeds and, for the full flavour, chop the chillies into the dish, using both the seeds and veins. Always taste a dish for heat as it is cooking. Sugar added to a dish that is too hot with chillies, tends to temper the heat of the food.

Most peppers are prepared by discarding the pith and the seeds before cooking or serving cold in salads or side dishes. Some cooks prefer to skin peppers before preparation, and peppers are ideal for stuffing. Capsicum peppers are most commonly used for stuffing, but poblanos, pasillas and mulatos are all suitable. If the peppers are to be skinned before stuffing, they should be grilled or charred. The peppers or chillies should be placed under a hot grill, where they blister. They should be turned to ensure scorching of most of the skin, which makes them easier to peel. Charring gives the peppers a smoky flavour and a sweet, juicy texture. Peppers can also be prepared for skinning by frying them in hot fat in a deep-fryer. Place peppers in a polythene bag for 15 minutes before removing the skin. This enhances their flavour.

Cayenne Pepper

Several varieties of chilli, including the very hot Cayenne chilli, are dried, ground and blended to make Cayenne pepper. Occasionally, other spices, seeds and salt are added so that cayenne pepper can range from dark red to golden brown. A Cayenne sauce can also be made in the same way but with the addition of vinegar.

Chilli Pastes and Salsas

Dried red chillies are ground to make chilli pepper, and some are steeped and heated in vegetable oil to create a pungent cooking oil. A chilli paste is made by pureeing a selection of chillies with a mixture of vinegar, sugar and salt. There are numerous recipes for chilli paste, the basis of many hot sauces. Thick chilli sauces are called pepian, or pipian, and the thinner table sauces made from chillies are called 'ajiaco' in the Spanish Caribbean, or 'salsa picante', the common word for hot sauce. Hot chilli sauces and salsa are made with a bewildering variety of ingredients. These might include a selection of herbs and spices, red, green or black peppercorns, onions and garlic, horseradish, ginger, sugar, molasses, honey, mustards, oils like peanut oil, sesame, olive, sunflower and palm oil, and a range of vinegars. Some might also include a variety of fruit and vegetables, like mango, papaya, pineapple, orange, lime, lemon, bananas, tomatoes, carrots, coconut and even sweet potato. Other lesser known ingredients might include tamarind, or grains of paradise, and some cooks even add rum, wines or sherry.

Chilli Powder

Chillies are ground to make chilli powder, which can be either neat or mixed with the additional flavouring of crushed spices, herbs and aromatic seeds such as cayenne, cumin and oregano. Chilli powder can vary in its heat, the hottest being that made from pure ground, small, bright red birds-eye chillies, providing a strong rust-red powder with a fiercely hot aroma and taste. Chilli powder is also made with smoked chillies. Small pointed peppers are dried and ground to make a Spanish version of Paprika, known as pimenton. Chilli salt is finely ground chilli powder mixed with sea salt, and used to rub into meat and fish prior to barbecuing or grilling. Chilli flakes are made in a similar way, from dried and crushed chillies and are often used in commercial products to aid preservation in such foods as sausages. Paprika is also a warm-flavoured, less pungent red chilli powder, known for its slightly sweet taste with a faint bitter after taste.

Achiote Powder

A mixture of ground spices, herbs, chillies and achiote, or annatto, combine to form this powder which adds colour and pungency to a variety of dishes. This powder is often mixed with lime juice and olive oil to make a marinade for fish and meat, before barbecuing or grilling. Achiote can come in paste or block form, when it is dissolved in grapefruit juice before using. Achiote is used to flavour fish, fowl or meat. The orange-red seeds of the Bixa tree are known as annatto and have a covering which produces a red or yellow vegetable dye, used for colouring foods and giving olive oil an orange tint.

Chilli Sauce Recipes

There are numerous recipes for chilli sauces, some of which can be fiery-hot, and others mysteriously mild yet warming. The heat of any sauce can be adjusted by limiting the number of chillies used. From Cuba to China, and from Trinidad to Thailand, the variety and piquancy of local sauces vary across the world, as do the spices, herbs and other ingredients used. Here are some basic, classic examples of sauces with chillies.

ANCHO ADOBO

This sauce is ideal as a dip or used to enhance soups or stews.

12 dried Ancho chillies, sliced lengthways
1 fresh Habanero chilli, quartered
2 medium onions, finely sliced
6 cloves of garlic, finely sliced
4 tbsp tomato ketchup
1 tbsp tomato pureé
5 tbsp vinegar
1 tsp salt
3 cups water

Simmer all ingredients gently in water for around 50 minutes. Blend into a paste, which is used as a pickle or food additive.

MINT AND CHORISCO SALSA

This mildly hot, mint-flavoured sauce is ideal with lamb.

3 Chorisco chillies, seeded and chopped
1 large bunch of mint, de-stalked
juice of half lime
1 tbsp malt vinegar
2 tsp brown sugar
3 cloves garlic, crushed
1 anchovy
1 tsp olive oil

Blend ingredients to a paste in blender, adding water if needed.

RED CHILLI SAUCE

This is a sauce with relish, toned down by the taste of tomatoes.

6 fresh Jalapeno chillies, seeded and finely chopped
1lb tomatoes, blanched, seeded, skinned and chopped small
1 medium onion, finely chopped
2 garlic cloves, finely chopped
1 tsp ground coriander
2 tbsp brown sugar
1 tbsp wine vinegar
4 tbsp tomato ketchup
55ml (2 fl oz) maize oil
4 tbsp water

Fry onions and garlic in oil until soft. Pureé chillies and tomatoes with the water. Add the onions and the rest of ingredients and pureé. Simmer the mixture for 10 minutes and let cool. Pureé mixture again and serve.

GREEN CHILLI SAUCE

This sauce can be served with meat or fish, and has a fresh taste that tickles the palate.

6 fresh thin green chillies, seeded and chopped fine
1 tomato, blanched, skinned and chopped small
1 large onion, finely chopped
2 garlic cloves, finely chopped
1 tsp ground chilli
1/2 tsp ground coriander
1/2 tsp ground cumin
2 tbsp maize oil
300ml (12 fl oz) water
Pinch of salt

Fry onions and garlic in oil until soft. Add remaining ingredients and simmer for 30 minutes. Let cool and blend to a pureé.

YELLOW CHILLI SAUCE

This mild chilli sauce adds colour and a warming heat to any dish.

  12 yellow Cera chillies
  1 tbsp sunflower oil
  1 tbsp white wine vinegar
  1 tbsp salt

Boil the chillies in 1 1/2 pints of water for 5 minutes. Cool, and halve the chillies, discarding the seeds. Pureé chillies, oil, vinegar and salt in blender.

NUTTY CHIPOTLE SAUCE

Pumpkin seeds and medium chillies make a good sauce for grills and pasta.

8 dried Chipotle chillies, seeded and soaked
1 medium onion, finely chopped
2 large tomatoes, chopped
2 tbsp toasted pumpkin seeds
pinch of salt and pepper

Sauté the onion, then blend all ingredients together in blender.

PIQUIN AND PEANUT SAUCE

The heat of the Piquin chillies are toned down by peanut butter. This sauce goes well with chicken.

10 Piquin chillies, seeded and finely chopped
1 large onion, finely chopped
4 cloves garlic, finely chopped
3 large tomatoes, chopped
6 tbsp peanut butter
2 tsp lime juice
50g (2oz) butter
1/2 cup coconut milk

Sauté the onion and garlic in butter. Add tomatoes, chillies and peanut butter. Stir whilst cooking for 5 minutes. Pour mixture into blender and add lime juice. Blend, adjusting consistency with coconut milk.

HABANERO SAUCE

The heat of this sauce can be increased with added Tabasco.

6 fresh Habanero chillies, seeded and finely chopped
110g (4oz) papaya, finely chopped
3 medium onions, finely chopped
3 garlic cloves, finely chopped
1/2 tsp turmeric
3 tbsp malt vinegar
1 tsp salt
1 tsp Tabasco sauce
1/4 tsp allspice
1 tsp annatto flavoured oil
1 tsp brown sugar
1 tbsp red wine
1 tbsp sherry
1 tbsp tomato pureé
1 tbsp Old rum

Bring to boil all ingredients in a saucepan, stirring constantly. Reduce heat and simmer for 5 minutes. Let sauce cool, and blend to a smooth pureé.

SALSA BORRACHA

This is called 'drunken' sauce, as rum replaces the usual stock.

    6 Ancho chillies, chopped
    1/4 bottle Gold rum
    2 tomatoes, peeled and chopped
    1 small onion, finely chopped
    1 clove garlic
    1/2 tsp salt
    1/4 tsp brown sugar
    1 tbsp olive oil

Soak the chillies in the rum overnight. Pureé all ingredients, except oil, in blender. Add the mixture to hot oil in pan. Fry, stirring occasionally, for 5 minutes.

CHIPOTLE SALSA

This smoked Jalapeno sauce is ideal on meat, when mixed with tomato paste.

    4 Chipotle chillies
    1 clove garlic, charred
    1 tsp olive oil
    150ml (5 fl oz) water
    5 tbsp tomato paste

Blend all ingredients together, except tomato paste. Then fry the mix in the oil for 5 minutes, Stir in tomato paste.

Sauce for the Goose

"Pyes, gelyes, tartes and cremes,
Sucking pigs served as a dish,
A fortnight fed with dates and Muscadine."
From an Old French Menu.

The link between food and sex was explicit in 18th century France: prostitutes would devise the most luxurious dishes and extravagant sauces to attract their customers. They would advertise their 'petits soupers', or menus, to seduce their clients from the attentions of competing whores. To these dishes, they added spices and herbs that were designed to inflame their client's passion, such as ginger, chillies, pepper, exotic spices and sometimes Spanish Fly. The French prostitutes' sauces were often known as 'quelques choses'.

These dishes were prepared in special kitchens, known as 'salons de preparation', where not only food was cooked, but all manner of exotic aphrodisiacs were also concocted. The Marquis de Sade was a particular devotee of the resulting naked feasts, and describes them in exquisite detail in his '120 Days of Sodom'. The French statesman, Tallyrand de Perigord (1754-1838), once said that there were two things uppermost in his life, "to give good dinners and to keep on fair terms with women." The boudoir women of Paris would have known exactly how he could have achieved the latter, by providing the ultimate in food, and intimate in sex, and being able to match the sauce, or aphrodisiac, to the occasion!

As with all the sauces and aphrodisiac ingredients contained in this book, no guarantee can be made of their effectiveness. At the end of the day it is imagination and desire that will impart the most vitality to a relationship. Aphrodisiacs are made for two.

Remember: a lone tango is no tango!

Flavour and Fragrance

Apart from using a single herb or spice to flavour a particular food, another favourite way of imparting flavour, or a combination of flavours, is with ready-prepared sauces. Some sauces are made with just one herb or spice ingredient, the most common being parsley sauce, generally used for fish dishes, mint dishes (mainly reserved for lamb) and caper sauce, more often used as a meat accompaniment. Many sauces, marinades and garnishes are made with a complicated variety of ingredients, carefully selected to enhance, and bring out the flavour of a particular food or mixture of foods.

The most commonly used sauces are based around the classic white sauce, which has many variations; 'Sauce Tartare', a combination of gherkins, capers and parsley, and often used with fish dishes; and 'mayonnaises', of which there are many variations. Some sauce recipes are well established, with familiar names like Bearnaise sauce, in which tarragon and parsley are the main flavourings, or Hollandaise sauce, which takes its flavour from lemon, pepper and vinegar. Chaudfroid sauce combines the flavours of bay, parsley, onions and pepper.

There are also sauces like salad cream or dressings, which are designed especially for salads and cold dishes, and they usually comprise of a smooth mixture of extracts of mustard, egg and oils. Some variations might be based on cheese, herbs, garlic or mint, depending on which meal it accompanies. Then there is horseradish sauce, traditionally served with beef and even oyster sauce and soy sauce, used mainly in Oriental cookery.

There are also the familiar bottled sauces, like tomato sauces, ketchup or catsup and the brown sauces, which have a multitude of ingredients combined into a liquid pureé. The variety of chilli sauces and chilli preparations are legion and range as much in ingredients as they do in heat. Many of these are almost pure chilli, combined into a medium to create a sauce. Others are coarser and are made as side dishes, dips and relishes. Commonly found in most kitchens are a variety of marinades and relishes and there are numerous cook-in sauces, designed to impart flavour, usually to meat or fish whilst it is cold. They are also used in tenderising and can double as a basting sauce once the marinade is completed.

Many sauces are meant to be used as a cold side accompaniment to a meal, and typical of these are the vast range of chutneys that have a number of main ingredients, including fruits and vegetables. A prime example would be mango chutney, which is a combination of mangoes, spices and sugar products. Pickles can be more complicated, one of the more common being mustard pickle or piccalilli. Lime pickle typically combines limes, mustard seeds, paprika, turmeric, fenugreek, onion powder, chillies, vinegar and oil.

In many cookery recipes a mixture of dried crushed herbs known as 'fine herbes' are often used in casseroles and stews. A substitute for fine herbes is the French 'bouquet garni', the term for a mixture of dried herbs bunched together in a small muslin cloth and used in soups, stews and sauces. The bouquet garni is added whilst cooking, during which time the flavour infuses into the dish, and it is then removed before serving. A typical bouquet garni would consist of parsley, thyme, and a bay leaf. Where whole bay leaves are used loose in cookery, they should be removed after cooking.

Sauces for Fish and Seafood

Traditionally, certain sauces are accepted as being ideally suited to particular fish and seafood dishes. Many of these classic sauces are based on the White, or Bechamel Sauce. This sauce was said to have been invented in France in the late 17th century, when Louis de Bechamel, Marquis de Nointel and a steward in the house of King Louis XIV introduced it to the royal table for the first time. Bechamel sauce is easily made and is used as the basis of the more exotic sauces, such as those that follow. Most of the sauces are then served with poached, baked or steamed firm white fish, with the exception of herring roe sauce, which is the classic sauce for grilled herrings. The other exception is tartare sauce, which is not based on the Bechamel sauce and is served cold with seafood. Otherwise, the choice of fish that is served with each sauce is a matter of personal taste.

BECHAMEL SAUCE

50g (2oz) plain flour
50g (2oz) unsalted butter
1 small onion
4 cloves
6 peppercorns
570ml (1 pint) milk

Stud the onion with the cloves, place in a pan with the milk and add the peppercorns and bay leaves. Bring the milk slowly to the boil. Remove from the heat at boiling point and let stand for 10 minutes. Strain the liquid into a bowl and set aside. Heat butter in a frying pan until it is foaming and slowly stir the flour in to create a paste. Bit by bit stir in the milk mixture, whisking constantly and stir until the mixture is smooth, bringing the sauce to the boil. Pass the mixture through a sieve to eliminate lumps.

PARSLEY SAUCE

570ml (1 pint) Bechamel Sauce
2 tbsp fresh parsley, finely chopped

Add the parsley to the sauce and heat over a gentle heat, so that the flavours of the herb infuse throughout the Bechamel.

TARTARE SAUCE

2 eggs, hard boiled
1 egg yolk
1 tsp capers, finely chopped
1 tsp fresh parsley, finely chopped
1 tsp chives, finely chopped
1/2 pint maize oil
1 tbsp vinegar
1/4 tsp salt and freshly ground black pepper, mixed together

Remove the yolks from the hard boiled eggs and rub them through a sieve. Stir in the raw egg yolk. Stirring slowly, add the oil a drop at a time. Press one egg white through the sieve and into the sauce. Stir in the vinegar and add the parsley and chives. Add seasoning and capers.

EGG SAUCE

570ml (1 pint) Bechamel Sauce
3 eggs, hard boiled
1/4 tsp salt and freshly ground pepper mixed together

Remove the yolks from the hard boiled eggs. Heat the sauce until it is just below boiling point, stirring regularly and reduce the heat. Press the egg whites through a sieve into the sauce. Stir well and increase heat to below boiling.

MORNAY (CHEESE) SAUCE

570ml (1 pint) Bechamel Sauce
6 oz hard cheese, finely grated
1/2 tsp mustard powder
2 tsp milk

Mix the mustard powder to a paste using the milk. Heat the Bechamel sauce to just below boiling point, stirring frequently. Stir in the mustard mixture and then add the cheese and heat gently until it melts. Stir thoroughly.

VELOUTE SAUCE

570ml (1 pint) Bechamel Sauce
1/4 tsp lemon juice
1/4 tsp salt and freshly ground pepper mixed together
1 egg yolk, lightly beaten
2 tbsp double cream

Mix cream and egg yolk together. Heat the sauce and stir in the cream and egg mix. Add the lemon juice and seasoning. Heat the sauce but do not boil.

ANCHOVY SAUCE

570ml (1 pint) Bechamel Sauce
25g (1oz) unsalted butter
3 tbsp double cream
1 tbsp anchovy essence

Heat the sauce until below boiling point. Melt the butter into the sauce. Add the cream and anchovy essence while stirring. Simmer for around five minutes without letting the sauce come to the boil.

HERRING ROE SAUCE

570ml Bechamel Sauce
225g (8oz) soft herring roe
50g (2oz) butter
1/2 tbs mixed mustard
1 tsp lemon juice

Cook the roes in half the butter over a low heat. Press the roes into the heated sauce through a sieve and then stir in the mustard and lemon juice. Melt the rest of the butter into the sauce and serve with herring.

The classic sauce for shellfish and in particular prawns is cocktail sauce, which is a mixture of different sauces and is commonly used in Prawn Cocktail or with shrimp.

The classic sauce for shellfish and in particular prawns is cocktail sauce, which is a mixture of different sauces and is commonly used in Prawn Cocktail or with shrimp.

PRAWN COCKTAIL SAUCE (I)

2 tbsp double cream
1/2 pint mayonnaise
1 tbsp tomato ketchup
1 tsp Worcestershire sauce
1/4 tsp Tabasco sauce
1 tsp mixed salt and pepper
1/4 tsp cayenne pepper
2 limes, quartered
1 tsp paprika.

Combine all ingredients except for paprika together in a bowl. Beat until smooth and evenly coloured. Spoon mixture over prawns, shrimp or lobster tails. Garnish with paprika and limes.

PRAWN COCKTAIL SAUCE (2)

3 tbsp mayonnaise
3 tbsp tomato ketchup
3 tbsp cream
1 tsp Worcestershire sauce
1 tsp lime or lemon juice
1/4 tsp Tabasco sauce
1/4 tsp paprika

Combine ingredients together as a pureé in a blender.

Cocktail Sauce with prawns and shrimp is usually served with a sprig of parsley and a slice or two of lime or lemon as a garnish to squeeze over the seafood.

Sauces for Meat, Poultry and Game

Some sauces are ideally suited for a certain meat, although it is a matter of taste. Traditionally, mint sauce is the classic accompaniment to lamb, cranberry sauce perfectly complements turkey, apple sauce is best with pork, and beef gets its kicks from horseradish sauce.

MINT SAUCE

2 tbsp fresh mint, finely chopped
2 tsp caster sugar
4 tbsp vinegar
1 tbsp boiling water

Pound the mint with the sugar in a mortar. Set aside for 30 minutes. Add boiling water to dissolve the sugar and finally, stir in the vinegar.

CRANBERRY SAUCE

225g (8oz) fresh cranberries, de-stalked and washed
225g (8oz) caster sugar
1/2 pint boiling water

Boil the cranberries in the water for 5 minutes. Mash the mixture through a sieve and discard skins. Add the sugar and bring the mixture to the boil. Stir until sugar is completely dissolved.

BROWN SAUCE

1 onion, chopped
1 carrot, finely sliced
2 rashers bacon, chopped
25g (1oz) flour
1 tsp tomato pureé
3/4 pint stock
25g (1oz) dripping
1 tsp tomato pureé
1/2 tsp salt and freshly ground pepper mixed together

Sauté onion and carrots with bacon in dripping until brown. Stir in the flour and cook gently for 15 minutes. Slowly add the stock and cook gently for 15 minutes. Slowly add the stock, stirring well until smooth. Add the tomato pureé and season with the salt and pepper mix. Bring to the boil and simmer for 30 minutes. Strain the sauce through a sieve.

Apple sauce is the ideal accompaniment to duck, pork or goose.

APPLE SAUCE

450g (1lb) cooking apples, peeled, cored and sliced
25g (1oz) butter
25g (1oz) caster sugar
rind of quarter of a lemon
4 cloves

Stew apples, cloves and lemon rind in a little water for 10 minutes. Stir in the sugar and press into a pureé through a sieve. Add the butter and reheat.

*The root of the horseradish is peppery and is often used in vinegars,
chutneys and pickles. Horseradish sauce is a traditional accompaniment
to beef and is usually served cold. There are several recipes for
horseradish sauces, some made with herbs and others which are served
hot.*

HORSERADISH SAUCE

3 tbsp freshly grated horseradish
1 tsp mixed mustard
1 tsp sugar
1 tsp lemon juice
1/2 tsp salt
1/2 pint double cream, whipped
1/4
2 tsp vinegar

Mix all ingredients except the cream, thoroughly in a bowl. Fold in
the cream and serve.

Bread sauce is traditionally served hot with chicken or turkey.

BREAD SAUCE

1 onion, quartered
50g (2oz) fresh white breadcrumbs
1/2 pint milk
10g butter
1 bay leaf
1 tbs cream
1/4 tsp salt and freshly ground pepper mixed

Bring milk, onion and bay leaf almost to the boil. Cover and set aside for 30 minutes. Strain into a pan. Add breadcrumbs and stir well. Add butter, salt and pepper and then stir in the cream.

Fresh tomato sauce is traditionally served with veal or chicken, but can also accompany fish dishes.

TOMATO SAUCE

450g (1lb) ripe tomatoes, quartered
1 tbsp flour, mixed with 3 tbsp water
1 tsp caster sugar
50g (2oz) butter
1 rasher bacon, chopped
1 onion, finely chopped
1 carrot, finely sliced
1/2 pint chicken stock
1/2 tsp salt and freshly ground black pepper mixed together
1/2 tsp lemon juice

Fry bacon in half of the butter for 2 minutes and add onion and carrot. Sauté for 5 minutes, add tomatoes, cover and cook for 5 minutes. Stir in the stock then stir in the flour mix. Add salt and pepper, lemon juice and sugar. Cover and simmer for 30 minutes. Let cool and then press through a sieve, discarding the pips and skins. Reheat the sauce and stir in rest of butter.

Mustard sauce can be used for fish and seafood dishes, and for some meat dishes. This recipe for mustard sauce uses the basic Bechamel white sauce as a base.

MUSTARD SAUCE

570ml (1 pint) Bechamel Sauce
1/2 tsp mustard powder
1 small chilli
2 egg yolks
6 oz double cream
3 tsp malt vinegar
1/2 tsp lemon juice

Make a paste with the mustard and vinegar. Mix paste and lemon juice into the sauce and add the chilli. Bring to the boil and remove chilli. Reduce heat and stir in egg yolks and cream. Heat sauce to just under boiling point.

One universally known spicy sauce that can be served with meat, chicken, fish or eggs is curry sauce.

CURRY SAUCE

1 onion, chopped
1 apple, peeled, cored and chopped
1 garlic clove
1 tsp black treacle
1 tbsp chutney
1/2 bay leaf
25g (1oz) flour
25g (1oz) butter
1/2 tsp caraway seeds
1/2 tsp cumin seeds
1 tsp cardamom seeds
1 tsp curry paste
3 tbsp curry powder
1/2 tsp salt
1/2 tsp lemon juice
1 tbsp desiccated coconut

Fry onion and apple in butter for 5 minutes. Add curry powder and cook for 3 minutes, stirring. Stir in the flour. Pound the bay, cardamom, cumin, caraway and garlic together. Stir into the mixture.

Stir in the coconut, curry paste and salt and add the stock. Bring to the boil, covering and simmering for 20 minutes. Stir in the treacle, chutney and lemon juice. Simmer for 15 minutes, stirring occasionally. Strain the sauce through a sieve.

Finally, the saucy sting in the tail is called Creole sauce and this hot concoction can be made as mild or as hot as one desires, depending on the number of chillies used. It goes well with almost all foods, especially steaks, chops, sausages and omelettes.

CREOLE SAUCE

2 green bell peppers, seeded and finely chopped
2 onions finely sliced
2 hot chillies, seeded and finely chopped
25g (1oz) butter
225g (8oz) tinned tomatoes
1 tsp caster sugar
1 tbsp cornflour
1/2 tsp salt and freshly ground pepper, mixed together

Sauté the onions, pepper and chillies in butter for 10 minutes. Add tomatoes, salt, pepper and sugar. Bring to the boil and simmer for 5 minutes. Make a paste with cornflour and a little water. Stir into the sauce and cook while stirring until it thickens.

Sweet Seduction

In preparing the ultimate aphrodisiac meal for one's lover, it is very important to make sure there is room for dessert, as the energising effects of sugar, sensual fruits and chocolate are undoubtedly the best prelude to the bedroom. Here are a few seductive saucy suggestions.

ROMANTIC SAUCE (CLARET SAUCE)

2 tbsp redcurrant jelly
1 tbsp sugar
rind of 1 lemon, grated
1 tsp arrowroot, mixed in 1 tbsp water
1/4 pint water
2 tbsp claret

Bring jelly, sugar, rind and 1/4 pint of water to the boil. Simmer for 8 minutes, then add arrowroot, cook until clear. Add wine and serve.

TART SAUCE (MARMALADE SAUCE)

3 tbsp marmalade
2 strips lemon peel
1 tbsp sugar
1 tbsp cornflour, mixed in 1 tbsp water
1 pint water

Bring all ingredients to the boil except arrowroot mixture. Simmer for around 6 minutes, then thicken with cornflour. Strain sauce through a sieve, then re-heat and serve.

DELIGHTFUL SAUCE (DAMSON SAUCE)

225g (8oz) damsons, stoned
4 tbsp sugar
275ml (10 fl oz) water

Cook damsons with water and sugar until they are soft. Leave to cool, then rub damsons through a strainer. Return mixture to heat and serve hot.

LAID-BACK SAUCE (FUDGE SAUCE)

150g (6oz) sugar
110g (4oz) butter
50g (2oz) soft brown sugar
220ml (8 fl oz) evaporated milk
1 tbsp gold rum

Over a moderate heat, cook the sugar and the butter. Stir whilst cooking, until butter and sugars have dissolved. Stir in the evaporated milk and bring to the boil. Boil for around 5 minutes. Remove from the heat and stir in the rum. It is at this point that some sauce-lovers prefer to crumble on illicit substance into this sauce, to which it is ideally suited.

FRUITY SAUCE (STRAWBERRY SAUCE)

450g (1lb) strawberries, hulled and washed
150g (6oz) caster sugar
juice of 1 lemon
2 tbsp Kirsch

Select the largest and finest-looking strawberry and set aside. Rub the rest of the strawberries through a sieve into a bowl. Add sugar, lemon juice and Kirsch and stir. When the sugar has dissolved, chill sauce for 1 hour. When serving, place the selected strawberry erect on top of sauce.

ARDENT SAUCE (MARSHMALLOW SAUCE)

10 marshmallows, cut into small pieces
110g (4oz) sugar
2 tbsp milk
1 egg white, beaten until stiff
1/2 tsp vanilla essence

Dissolve sugar in milk over moderate heat. Bring to the boil then simmer for 5 minutes, stirring. Add the marshmallows and stir until dissolved. When mixture thickens, remove from heat. Fold the egg into the mixture. Stir in vanilla essence then serve.

SUGGESTIVE SAUCE (Banana Sauce)

3 bananas
juice of 1 lemon
2 tbsp maraschino liqueur
50g (2oz) sugar
6 tsp arrowroot
6 tbsp water

Peel bananas and slice one lengthways. Slice the remaining bananas thinly, and one of the halves. Combine lemon juice, water and maraschino in a pan. Add sugar and dissolve it in mixture over low heat. Mix the arrowroot into a paste with a little cold water. Stir into the hot mixture and whisk until clear. Add slices of banana, place half a banana on sauce and serve hot.

FRUITS OF LOVE (Apricot Spice Sauce)

110g (4oz) dried apricots, finely chopped
juice of 1 orange
1/2 cup apple juice
2 tbsp clear honey
2 tsp cornflour
1 tsp ground ginger powder
1 tsp ground cinnamon powder
1 tbsp sweet vermouth
2 tbsp water

Pour apple juice and orange juice over apricots in a pan. Bring to boil and simmer for 10 minutes. Stir in regularly, push through strainer, reserve liquid and mush. Mix cornflour with the water into a paste. Add honey, ginger and cinnamon. Heat until mixture thickens, then add apricot liquid. Remove from heat and add apricot mush and vermouth. Return to heat for 1 minute, then serve hot and chilled.

AFFECTIONATE SAUCE (Apricot Wine Sauce)

110g (4oz) dried apricots, finely chopped
3 tbsp apricot jam
1 tbsp clear honey
1 tsp Worcestershire sauce
1/2 tsp dark soy sauce
3 tbsp dry white wine

Add all ingredients in a pan. Cook, stirring until jam has melted, then serve hot.

GINGER SPICE SAUCE

1 onion, finely sliced
1 inch of fresh ginger root, finely sliced
2 tbsp light soy sauce
2 tbsp rice wine vinegar
juice of 1 orange
1/4 tsp allspice

Reduce all ingredients in blender until smooth sauce is obtained.

PAN'S SAUCE (CHOCOLATEY SAUCE)

50g (2oz) cocoa powder
175g (6oz) sugar
1/4 pint water

Over a low heat, dissolve sugar in the water. Bring to the boil and simmer for 2 mintues. Take off heat and stir in cocoa powder. Mix until smooth and leave to thicken.

SAUCE OF IMPULSE (Kahlua Chocolate Sauce)

110g (4oz) plain bitter chocolate
2 tbsp butter
2 tbsp double cream
1 tbsp sugar
2 tbsp vegetable oil
2 tbsp Kahlua

Combine all ingredients except for Kahlua in a pan. Heat, stirring regularly for 10 minutes. Add Kahlua, heat for 1 minute, then serve hot or cold.

SEDUCTION SAUCE (RASPBERRY AND CINNAMON SAUCE)

450g (1lb) fresh raspberries, washed
2 tbsp brown sugar
2 tsp cornflour
1 tbsp lemon juice
1/2 tsp cinnamon
1/4 tsp salt

Press half of raspberries through a sieve, discarding seeds. Add the sugar to the pulp and juice. Stir in lemon juice, cornflour, cinnamon and salt. Stir into a paste, then add the rest of the raspberries. In a pan, cook over medium heat until whole raspberries are soft. Serve hot.

PLEASURABLE SAUCE (ORANGE ROSEMARY SAUCE)

juice of 5 oranges
zest of 5 orange peels
1 cup sugar
1 tbsp fresh rosemary, finely chopped
3 tbsp water

Boil the water and add rosemary, leaving for 1 hour. Strain off water and keep. Add sugar to the rosemary water. Bring to the boil, and cook until sugar has melted. Add the orange juice and zest, and re-heat to boiling. Sieve the sauce, then thicken if required with a little cornflour.

DARK BROWN BODY SAUCE (DARK CHOCOLATE SAUCE)

110g (4oz) bitter chocolate, broken in pieces
110g (4oz) cooking chocolate
1 tbsp double cream
2 tsp dark brown sugar
1/4 tbsp butter
2 tbsp dark rum

Over a moderate heat, bring cream and sugar to the boil. Whisk, and when sugar dissolves, remove from heat. Add chocolates and return to heat. Remove from heat and stir in butter and rum. Whisk until smooth and serve warm or hot.

CUPID'S SAUCE (CHOCOLATE SAUCE)

1/2 cup milk chocolate powder
1 cup evaporated milk
1 tbsp golden syrup
1/2 tsp vanilla essence
2 tbsp butter

Mix the chocolate powder, milk and syrup in a pan. Stirring, bring to the boil over a moderate heat. Simmer for 5 minutes, then remove from heat. Add vanilla essence and butter. When the butter has melted, stir and serve.

FRESH SAUCE (CHERRY NUTMEG SAUCE)

450g (1lb) fresh cherries, stoned and washed
2 tbsp sugar
2 tbsp lemon juice
1 tbsp dry white wine
1/4 tsp allspice

Combine 3/4 of the cherries in pan with sugar, wine and lemon juice. Simmer for 15 minutes until fruit is soft. Let cool and pureé in a blender. Return to pan and add rest of cherries and allspice. Cook on low heat for 2 minutes, serve hot.

QUELQUES CHOSES SAUCE (CHOCOLATE CREAM SAUCE)

1/2 cup chocolate milk powder
1 cup evaporated milk
1 tbsp golden syrup
2 tbsp butter, melted
1/2 tsp vanilla essence

Mix milk powder, milk, chocolate and syrup in a pan. Bring to the boil, stirring, then simmer for 5 minutes. Remove from heat and stir in vanilla and butter. Serve hot.

EXCITEMENT SAUCE (CHOCOLATE MINT SAUCE)

12 chocolate mint wafers
1/2 pint cream

Over a pan of boiling water, melt the wafers in a small bowl. Stir slowly whilst adding the cream. Serve.

ORGIASTIC SAUCE (CHOCOLATE COINTREAU SAUCE)

3/4 lb dark dessert chocolate, grated
3/4 pint double cream
2 egg yolks
rind of 1 orange, grated
1 tbsp cointreau
2 tbsp water

Melt the chocolate with the water. Separately bring cream to just below boiling. Add chocolate to the cream, stirring well. Blend the sugar with the yolks, then add to the mixture. Add orange rind and stir in the cointreau. Stir over a low heat until sauce thickens.

SINFUL SAUCE (LEMONY SAUCE)

25g (1oz) butter, melted
110g (4oz) caster sugar
1 tbsp cornflour
rind of 1 lemon
3 tbsp lemon juice
1 cup water
1/4 tsp salt

Combine all ingredients except juice and butter. Mix well over a
low heat, stirring constantly. Bring to the boil until sauce thickens.
Remove from heat and add the butter and lemon juice.

RABELAISIAN SAUCE (Melba Sauce)

3 tsp cornflour
225g (8oz) fresh raspberries
3 tbsp redcurrant jelly
1 tsp lemon juice
1 tbsp water

Over a low heat, mash the raspberries with the jelly. When the fruit is soft, remove from heat. Mix a paste from the cornflour and water. Add paste to the fruit, then bring slowly to the boil. When sauce is thick, strain and add the lemon juice.

FERTILITY SAUCE (Custard Sauce)

1/2 pint milk
2 tbsp cornflour
25g (1oz) caster sugar
1 egg, lightly beaten
4 drops vanilla essence

Blend the cornflour into a paste with 1/4 of the milk. Heat the rest of the milk to just below boiling. Take off the heat and stir in the cornflour mix. Bring to the boil until sauce thickens. Simmer for 2 minutes then stir in the sugar, egg and vanilla. Strain and serve hot.

DIONYSIA'S SAUCE (Caramel Sauce)

75g (3oz) sugar
1/4 pint double cream, whipped lightly
4 tbsp cold water

Melt the sugar until golden brown. Take off heat. Very carefully add the water to the sugar. It will froth up and boil very quickly. When froth has subsided, replace on heat and stir. When a thin caramel is produced, set aside to cool. Add the caramel to the cream, and mix thoroughly.

STIMULATING SAUCE (Chocolate Pine Nut Sauce)

50g (2oz) pine nuts, finely chopped
1 tbsp grated dark chocolate
2 tbsp white wine vinegar
75g (3oz) sugar
25g (1oz) seedless raisins, finely chopped

Combine all ingredients together and cook for around 20 minutes.

BLUSHING SAUCE (ROSE WINE SAUCE)

4 tbsp Rosé wine
75g (3oz) caster sugar
juice and grated rind of 1 lemon
1/2 pint double cream
1/4 tsp cochineal
1 tbsp crystallised rose petals

Mix the wine with the lemon juice, rind, wine and sugar. Leave to stand overnight. Fold cream into the sauce, adding a little cochineal. Colour, stirring until a light pink. Whisk the mixture until soft and folding. Serve garnished with rose petals.

The Scent of Sex

"You may break, you may shatter the vase if you will,
But the scent of roses will hang around it still."
Thomas Moore (1179-1852)

Not only were the Ancients expert at producing aphrodisiac foods, they also explored the power of smell. They utilised the aromatic oils and essences from herbs and spices to allure members of the opposite sex and enhance the mood for lovemaking. The sense of smell is over ten thousand times more sensitive than the sense of taste and in many respects it is the least understood and researched of the five basic senses. However, there are just seven classifications of basic aromas, of which six are fundamentally pleasing, and even the seventh can be thought of as stimulating. They are: camphoraceous, ethereal, floral, minty, musky, pungent and putrid.

However, there is one other classification, which is central to the field of aphrodisia – pheromonal. It is the least tangible of the aroma classifications, in that rather than being perceived consciously through the nose, it is received on a subconscious level. Pheromones have found their way into a number of 'sex appeal' sprays, but they occur naturally in human sweat, and they undoubtedly play a crucial part in the chemistry of attraction. Pheromones are considered to be such powerful stimulants that some countries forbid their use in perfumes and cosmetic preparations. Aromas can stimulate basic instincts in the brain, such as hunger, thirst, aggression and arousal, and it is widely known that smells can have an ability to stir up memories – both pleasant and unpleasant in the brain.

In the 1860s, Augustin Galopin bravely suggested that redheads had the strongest smell of all women, exuding the odour of amber, while at the other end of the scale, blonde women had a pervasive odour of violets. He unfortunately neglected to include the scent profiles of men in his tome, 'La Parfum de la Femme'. Everyone has their own natural scent or odour, discernible even between identical twins, which explains why a perfume may smell appealing on one person and not on another: it is dependent on how one's own scent interacts with that of the perfume. This also explains why some aphrodisiacs will work for an individual and others will not. Garlic is an example of this – if one partner eats it and the other does not, then it can be unpleasant. However if both partake, the effects can be quite arousing.

The History of Natural Scents

The sensual connotations of scents and aromas have been known about since the dawn of time. Primitive Man were experts in the development and use of scents, perfumes, unguents, fragrances and aromatherapy, their main interest being to use these aromas in religious practices to appease and placate their deities.

Egyptian priests would employ pungent substances in religious and funerary practices over 5000 years ago, and Egyptian Royalty evolved a range of aromatic cosmetics and perfumes. The Middle East later became the centre of trade in aromatic spices and in this region the Queen of Sheba seduced King Solomon around 800BC with perfumes.

By 700BC, the Babylonians were scouring the known world for aromatics and the trade in spices and fragrances sparked off numerous political clashes. By 650BC the Phoenician trade in scents had extended the knowledge of this science throughout the Old World. The Greeks experimented heavily throughout the 4th century BC and discovered that the best way to put both men and women in the mood for love was massage and caresses with oils and essences. The massage is more sensual when there is the lubrication of oil and the aroma of essences, and they help to heighten awareness of the body and the desire for sex. A recent survey showed that women prefer to be massaged on their neck and backs, with their breasts and genitals being of secondary importance, whereas men predominantly prefer genital massaging and caressing, with the back and neck being of minor importance.

In the 1st century BC, Cleopatra, Queen of the Egyptians employed the sacred perfume, kyphi, to seduce Alexander the Great. It was a mixture of 16 herbs and as well as being used as perfume, it was often burned to appease the ancient Egyptian gods. Its ingredients were documented by the Greek writer Democritus long before Cleopatra's time and by Plutarch's day (50-120AD) kyphi had evolved almost into a sauce mixture. The recipe included steeping cinnamon, myrrh, honey, raisins, juniper, spikenard, saffron and henna in wine. This perfume was included in foods served before statues of the Egyptian god of Wisdom, Thoth, who was represented in the animal kingdom by the sacred Ibis, which were often fed by devotees outside the temple of Karnak.

In the ancient days of Greece, violets were used to scent wine and violet perfume was eventually developed by the process of maceration, which involved crushing the flowers with animal fat in order to extract the essence, which is oil soluble. Violets were the symbol of Athens, where they were widely grown on a commercial basis. In more recent times violet essence was used in cachous, or lozenges, which were used to sweeten the breath before lovemaking.

Rome took over from Greece as the centre for research and development of pleasing aromas, and it held supreme position between the 1st century BC through to the 5th Century AD. Alexander the Great is said to have remarked on the subtle scent of crushed lemongrass, which was imported from its native Ceylon. It is now a popular ingredient in many dishes, most notably in Thai cuisine. It is said to be the closest scent available to spikenard, which is featured in the 'all-time greats' list of aphrodisiacs below and is nowadays quite hard to obtain. There are three varieties of lemongrass, one of which is widely used in perfumes and scents.

Attar, or oil of roses, is one of the most expensive natural scents. The essential oil is known as 'absolute' and needs vast quantities of rose petals to produce just a few drops. Rose oil was not only used to scent Roman wines, but it was also the main ingredient of rose pudding and a number of love potions.

Some of the main aromatic stimuli come in the form of herbs, spices and substances like ambergris, which is produced by sperm whales. This grey, wax-like substance has a strong, musky odour and it is said to improve one's virility as well as increasing passion, sexual desire and pleasure. In 18th century France, lozenges of ambergris were chewed to sweeten the breath before amorous liaisons and Madame du Barry swore by its ability to inflame the ardour. Brillat-Savarin (1755-1828), the famous French gastronome prepared a restorative for Madame de Pompadour from chocolate and ambergris. For an elderly, flagging friend whose young wife needed regular satisfaction in bed, he recommended taking a concoction containing beef, the meat of an old cockerel, onions, carrots, parley, sugar and 20 grams of ambergris.

Anise, a plant native to Egypt, was commonly used in ancient incense recipes of the region and the boy-king Tutankhamun was buried with an astonishing 400 litres of perfume, at the time worth more than all the gold which packed his tomb. Also his internal organs were all preserved in aromatic unguents supposedly to ensure that the king would be favourably received by members of the opposite sex in the afterlife. Over in early Mexico, the Aztecs and Mayans used the vanilla-scented Cereus grandiflorus cactus in their boudoirs. The chestnut flower has also been used throughout history on account of the similarity its smell has to male sperm (the chemical composition of both is remarkably similar). The essence was used as a bath oil as well as in perfumes and scents. The Marquis de Sade commented on the effects of the chestnut blossom, and incidentally Socrates taught his scholars under wild chestnut trees.

The number of natural products appearing in perfumes and scents as well as food is legion. Bergamot, cinnamon, cloves, honey, juniper, lemon, lemongrass, mint, orange, rosemary, rose, saffron, vetivert and violets are all eaten as culinary ingredients either to lend a certain taste or for decorative effect. They are also among the essential ingredients of scents and perfumes. Some scent sources are not commonly used in cookery but are sometimes added to beverages or alternatively are added to edible aphrodisiac potions. These include ambergris, cedar oil, civet, cypress oil, frangipani, frankincense, geranium oil, henna, hyacinth oil, jasmine, lavender, musk, myrrh, patchouli, sandalwood, spermaceti and spikenard.

Other oils that are often used for aphrodisiac purposes include bergamot, which is said to help the course of love run smoothly. Cinnamon allegedly encourages the object of one's affections to reciprocate. Jasmine is thought to improve fertility and musk improves vitality and stamina, and is therefore the ingredient in many love philtres. It comes from the glands of the male musk deer and it is employed as a fixative in numerous perfumes as the most expensive product from the animal kingdom. Truffles are a known aphrodisiac food, but they also have a very pungent aroma, which is said to stimulate both sexes. Finally, Ylang ylang, known as the 'flower of flowers' is a widely used ingredient in a range of scents and perfumes.

Throughout history is has been impossible to describe aromas in the same way as tastes. Tastes are sweet, bitter, rich or bland but the smell of an aroma can only really be described by analogy. A perfume is either pleasant or unpleasant and can often be described by likening it to something edible. This shows a link between the olfactory glands in the nose and the taste buds – physiologically they are also linked in that they are both located near each other and are similar in their structures. In aphrodisiacs, the senses of smell and taste often converge.

A recipe for sexual disaster!

The following is a list of 20 ingredients which are considered to be the most powerful natural aphrodisiacs, a concoction of which would not only be the 'King of Sauces' but would probably render even the most ardent lover senseless through its power! The author strongly recommends avoiding many of these substances, not least as some are poisonous, and instead sticking to the tried and tested aphrodisiac – love.

Truffles – a natural source of pheromones, closest to those produced by humans.
Absinthe (poison) – a combination of wormwood, elecampane, marjoram and anise. Produces a euphoric state.
Yohombie tree bark – a powerful euphoric.
Kava kava – stimulating euphoric.
Ambergris – a noted sexual restorative. Note that sperm whales are an endangered species, and so this should not be used.
Cereus cactus juice – a sexual stimulant.
Chestnut flowers – to replicate the scent of male stimulation.
Chocolate – an aphrodisiac through the ages.
Damiana – an irritant herb that stimulates the sex organs.
Dita Seeds – genital stimulants on account of the chlorogenic acid, which is a known irritant.
Spanish Fly (poison) – a hallucinogenic that produces strong aphrodisiac responses.
Fo-ti-tieng – used by Indians as a sexual tonic.
Ginseng – proven to stimulate physical and sexual activity.
Guarana – slows the heart rate and promotes sexual longing.
Musk – sexually exciting and is known to arouse.
Nux Vomica – stimulates the nervous system.
Pussywillow bark oil – a proven sexual tonic.
Saw palmetto berries – stimulate the erogenous zones.
Ylang ylang oil – a relaxing alluring oil that prepares the mood for love.
Satyrion – this would be the final ingredient in the ultimate aphrodisiac, but the recipe was so closely guarded that its exact nature has been a constant source of dispute over the centuries and its origins lost in the mists of time.

Herbs for the Hots

*"Scorn not garlic like some men think
it only maketh man winke and drinke and stinke."*
Sir John Harrington, 1609

In this short praise of garlic, the 17th century poet has cunningly hinted at the aphrodisiac qualities of the bulb, for winking is often the prelude to a relationship – slightly illicit, somewhat lewd, and just a little naughty! Shakespeare also hints at the aphrodisiac nature of herbs in his play 'Romeo and Juliet'. "O! mickle is the powerful grace that lies – In herbs, plants, stones, and their true qualities." In the 'Merchant of Venice', the Bard puts herbs at the forefront of aphrodisia. "Media gather'd the enchanted herbs – That did renew old Aeson." Ever since ancient times, herbs and plant extracts have been used in potions and concoctions that were designed to stimulate sexual feelings, or enhance the sexual act.

ANGELICA

During the 14th century, plague swept through Europe, and the herb angelica (Archangelica officinalis) was thought to be a cure. Angelica oil, distilled from the roots and leaves, is used to treat indigestion, stomach disorders, rheumatism and chest infections. The root is also an excellent aid to digestion. The stem and leaves are usually preserved or crystallised and used in confectionery, and angelica is used in flavouring desserts and fruit. The oil distilled from angelica is also used in the preparation of liqueurs, such as vermouth. Considered to have the same effect on women as ginseng has on males, this herb (Archangelic officinalis, or Angelica archangelica) is aptly named 'angelic herb'. All parts of the plant are useful and it is thought to improve gynaecological functions. Angelica is one of the oldest plants to be used medicinally and as an aphrodisiac, and is rich in essential oils and plant hormones.

Angelica is associated with Michael the Archangel, and inhabitants of the port of Archangel, on the White Sea, attribute longevity to chewing and smoking angelica. This herb played an important part in ancient pagan Springtime rites, especially as a purifier. An ancient tonic can be made by boiling a handful of angelica root in a quart of water for three hours, then straining it and adding enough honey to make it into a syrup.

The 16th century herbalist, Culpeper, recommended infusions of angelica for menstrual problems and breast irritations. It is said to be a female sexual stimulant before, during and after menopause. A related plant is known as 'dong kwai' (Angelica polymorpha) in China, and is reputed to be a natural source of the female sex hormones and hence is a powerful aphrodisiac for women.

BASIL

There are 50 varieties of Basil, but only two are commonly used, Sweet Basil (Ocimum basilicum) and Bush Basil (Ocimum minimum). Basil is the traditional herb for tomato dishes, and basil vinegar can be made by infusing leaves in wine vinegar for two weeks. Basil is also a good ingredient in tomato pureé and tomato juice preparations. Medicinally, basil is used in a snuff concoction to clear headaches, as an aid to digestion and as a laxative. Basil is also used in rice, potato and egg dishes, and is a good additive in soups and stews. This sacred herb is indigenous to India, where it was dedicated to the deities Krishna and Vishnu. In Rome, this was the herb ascribed to Venus, the goddess of Love, and it was used in religious rites. Basil, with its warm fragrance and soothing effect, was also known as the 'King of Herbs' as its Greek name is 'basileus', the word for king. It was once considered so potent that some people would not eat it. Basil is an essential ingredient in many love potions, often combined with garlic, pine kernels, cheese, butter and olive oil. The tangy scent of basil is occasionally used in the preparation of some perfumes.

BAY

Bay, or Bay Laurel (Laurus nobilis), has many uses in the kitchen and is available in powdered form, and as whole, dried or fresh leaves. Bay is one of the ingredients of bouquet garni and combines well with many meat dishes as well as fish, and in soups, stews and casseroles. Besides its uses in the kitchen, the leaves are an appetite stimulant, as are the crushed or infused berries. Bay leaves are both a narcotic and a stimulant, and bay can be used in cures for colic and hysteria. The oil in its leaves and berries has a deep aroma and is also used in perfumes.

Known by the ancients as the 'noble herb', bay was once sacred to Apollo, and it was often used by Delphic priestesses in magical rites as an aphrodisiac. Described suggestively as 'warm and penetrating', bay oil, the leaves and its berries are all excitants and narcotics as they contain prussic acid, a volatile toxin. Culpeper makes numerous references to bay as being a herb which wards off any 'evils old Saturn [age] can do to the body of man', affirming its potency as an aphrodisiac. He also links the herb to women in labour, as it was also believed to assist abortionists.

BORAGE

Borage (Borage officinalis) is a mild herb with a fresh, cucumber flavour, and although its culinary uses are limited, it can be used to flavour desserts. It is a mild stimulant and mood enhancer, which can be used to reduce fevers and as a mild diuretic. As a tonic and blood purifier, it is thought to be effective in preparing for the act of love. The Celtic word for borage, borrach, means 'courage', which suggests that taking this herb bolsters the spirit. It used to be used in cosmetic baths to improve the complexion and for its cooling effects. The blue, five-pointed flowers look like stars, and are often portrayed in religious pictures of the Madonna.

CAMOMILE

Camomile (Matricaria recutita) is a foot-high plant with sweet smelling white flowers, and its flowers are used to relieve tension, nervous problems, anxiety and sleeplessness, all of which can be causes of impotence and other sexual difficulties. An antiseptic blue-tinged oil is produced from the camomile, which stimulates the immune system and helps heal inflammation. This bitter herb was used for centuries as an anti-inflammatory in reducing temperatures during fevers. A medicinal digestive tea is also made from this distinctive, aromatic herb.

CHICORY

Once known as Succory, chicory (Cichorium intybus) can grow up to six foot, and the leaves and roots have a bitter quality. Chicory is used in salads and as a vegetable, and also in some medicinal preparations. Ground, dried chicory is also used as an additive to coffee or sometimes as a substitute for coffee. Chicory has been used in magic potions to cure frigidity in women.

CHIVES

The grass-like leaves of the pink-flowering chives (Allium schoeno-prasum) are used in the kitchen in the same way as spring onions, as they also belong to the onion family. Chives are used for their delicate onion flavour in soups, salads, omelettes and sauces. Chives are also a particularly good addition to mashed potatoes and to meat dishes. As the leaves contain iron, they are thought to help in stomach and kidney disorders, as well as in fortifying the blood – perhaps those wishing to be the most red-blooded of lovers should eat a lot of chives!

CRESS

There are three types of cress – watercress, garden cress and rocket. All have a slightly bitter, warming taste and are rich in vitamins. The name of rocket suggests its aphrodisiac qualities. Rocket cress (Eruca satvia) was dedicated to Priapus, the Roman god of Generation and Fructation, son of Venus and Bacchus. The Roman writers, Pliny, Ovid and Martial, all testified to the erotic powers of rocket. It has long been known for its aphrodisiac qualities, and the Persians took a preparation of rocket seed to promote male erection. It is said that a group of monks once ravished all the women of their village after quaffing a draught made from rocket.

Watercress is the larger leaf variety, and is an aquatic plant, mostly eaten raw as a garnish with salads. The fine stemmed garden variety, commonly called cress, has small leaves and is also used in salads.

DILL

Dill (Anthum graveolens) grows to 18 inches and has feathery leaves which are pungently aromatic, and similar to anise in quality and flavour. An infusion of the leaves is said to soothe the stomach and stimulate the system. The light brown, aromatic seeds are also used in flavouring savouries and eases digestion. Chopped dill leaves go well with fish dishes and cucumber, and it is also used in making dill pickles and dill cucumbers. Dill is used to flavour a number of sauces, to add piquancy to pickles and chutneys, vegetable and meat dishes. Widely used in magical potions and aphrodisiacs, dill is similar in appearance to fennel and has a flavour that is often compared to caraway.

Dill is used to stimulate the system, and dill seeds can be chewed to sweeten the breath prior to love-making. It is documented by Culpeper as an ingredient which is a 'provoker of terms', a reference to its potency in love potions. As fish and seafood are associated with aphrodisiacs, it is no coincidence that dill is one of the ideal herbs to accompany crabs, prawns, white fish and oily fish like mackerel. Dill is also commonly used in vinegars and spicy pickles, like those made with the suggestive gherkin and cucumber.

FENNEL

Fennel (Foeniculum vulgare) is an ancient culinary and medicinal herb, adding aroma to desserts, breads and cheese dishes, and brings out the flavour in meat dishes, pickles, sauces and curry powders. This herb can be made into a tea, used in eye compresses, and is a fine remedy for wind and indigestion. Fennel's feathery leaves go well with any fish dishes, and an infusion of the leaves can relieve sore eyes. The leaves have a slightly bitter taste, which is said to excite the nervous system, particularly in the region of the lower abdomen. Fennel seeds are also used as a flavouring and can be chewed to aid digestion. Fennel bulb has a sweet anise flavour and is eaten as a vegetable. The plant contains the essential oil, anethol, and an infusion of fennel and vervain is said to be a powerful aphrodisiac. Fennel, because of its feathery leaves, is known in Italy as 'finnochio', another term for a homosexual, and it has a tradition of being associated with snakes, yet another sexual symbol.

FENUGREEK

This herb is a member of the pea family, and can be used as a vegetable, although it has a bitter flavour. Usually, it is just the small seeds that are used as a traditional additive to fish dishes. Fenugreek contains an oestrogen-like chemical which can stimulate sexual appetite in women, but it is also a uterine stimulant that encourages menstruation and should not be used by pregnant women.

GARLIC

An indispensable ingredient in numerous dishes world wide, garlic (Allium sativum) is originally a native of Asia. It figures heavily in many recipes of the former Spanish colonies, and is a major ingredient in a vast number of sauces. A member of the same family as the lily, onion, chives, shallot and leek, the garlic bulb grows underground and consists of a cluster of cloves, held together with a papery skin. When crushed, the garlic clove releases an acrid oil, an important ingredient in many sauces and dressings, and for making garlic butter. Many savoury dishes contain garlic, either whole, chopped, crushed or mashed. Garlic oil, which basically includes olive oil, lemon juice and salt, plus pounded garlic, is widely used in Mediterranean and Caribbean cookery. The cloves of garlic have a sharply pungent smell and flavour, and are used as an antiseptic and a medicine in treatments of digestive disorders, respiratory complaints and high blood pressure. It is also said to be an anticoagulant, an antibacterial and an aphrodisiac. It lowers the blood cholesterol levels, and the sulphides contained in garlic are thought to prevent some cancers. Those who do not add garlic to their meals will soon experience the anti-social qualities of the garlic on the breath of those who do! Parsley is the best antidote to the smell of garlic.

Garlic contains a high level of Vitamin B1, which helps the body convert food into energy, and Vitamin C, which produces adrenaline and hormones that boost the system. Ancient Greeks dedicated garlic to their goddess of Enchantment, Hecate, and the ancient Romans attributed magical powers to garlic, which they used in numerous aphrodisiac sauces. Pliny describes quantities of garlic being beaten with coriander and infused with wine, to be drunk at orgies. A particular recipe for one aphrodisiac was a concoction made with garlic cloves, pine nuts, butter, basil and cheese. It is no coincidence that the Romans used garlic in aphrodisiac preparations and sexual applications, as it has both antiseptic and germicidal qualities – precautions which may have been essential considering the sexual proclivities of the ancient Romans.

JUNIPER

The Latin name for this tree is Juniperis communis, and indicates that it is part of the cypress family. The berry's oil is used in the treatments of gout, rheumatism, liver and kidney complaints, and as a cleanser to the system, and in the ancient practices of magic, juniper was used in love potions. The berries flavour gin and are infused in water to make a medicinal tea. The berries are also used to flavour game, poultry and meat dishes, and are added to marinades for pork and lamb dishes. They are usually crushed before use, and often added to stews.

LEMON BALM

Lemon balm (Melissa officinalis) was once called the elixir of life, and the oil from the plant is used to reduce tension, headaches, migraines and anxiety. It is also used in the treatment of asthma, high blood pressure and indigestion. It imparts a delicate lemony flavour to dessert dishes. Also known as Balm, it lives up to its name by symbolising pleasantry, being calming and soothing, and having the fragrance of lemon. Balm, itself, is a substance obtained from the herb Melissa, a form of mint plant. Fragrant and medicinal, balm was traditionally used in soothing unguents and aromatic lotions for anointing. In 1611, Carmelite monks prepared a concoction known as 'Carmalite Water', which was used as a cordial and perfume. This was a thinly disguised potency-inducing draught as it contained lemon balm, as told by members of the London Dispensary, to 'renew youth, and relieve languishing nature'. The eight ingredients included measures of balm in flower, coriander seed, cloves, cinnamon, nutmeg, angelica roots, lemon peel and lashings of 'spirits of wine'. The London Dispensary of 1696 recommended taking essence of balm in Canary wine, every morning!

MARJORAM

Sweet Marjoram (Origanum magorana) is widely used in sauces, salads, vinegars, omelettes, soups and stews. Marjoram can also add flavour to fish and cheese dishes. It is a comforting herb, used for indigestion and for tension headaches and is also a medicine for high blood pressure and sore muscles. In herbal medicine, the highly aromatic marjoram is well known as a remedy for narcotic poisons, and as a sexual nerve tonic. Culpeper discretely says that marjoram is "excellent for the brain and other parts of the body". Marjoram was also one of the seven herbal ingredients in 'Carmelite Water', and was also in the preparation known as the 'Vinegar of the Four Thieves'. Marjoram was also used extensively in perfumes and scents from the earliest of times.

MINTS

There are seven types of mint, three of which are more commonly used in culinary concoctions. These include Spearmint (Mentha spicata), and Pennyroyal (Mentha pulegium). Spearmint aids digestion, and is used in a medicinal drink and to stimulate the appetite. This mint is used in sauces and jellies to flavour meats, as are the leaves of the peppermint, which produces an important essential oil that is mildly antiseptic. Peppermint tea, mint julep and creme de menthe are among the numerous uses for this mint. The pungent Pennyroyal was once used as a purgative for the blood. Peppermint and other mints are of course widely used to sweeten the breath, especially prior to amorous meetings.

OREGANO

Oregano (Origanum onites) is a branch of the marjoram family and is more commonly known as pot marjoram, but it is wild marjoram that is usually called oregano. It is generally used with tomatoes and meat sauces. Oregano has a mild tranquillising effect, which can be relaxing prior to lovemaking, and it also promotes menstruation.

PARSLEY

Parsley (Petroselinum crispium) is an antidote to the smell of garlic and also reduces uric acid. It contains amounts of Vitamin A, potassium, calcium and iron. Parsley is more commonly used as a culinary decoration, but it does have a distinct flavour of its own which comes out in parsley sauce, usually used with fish. Parsley tea is a good source of iron, drunk as a tonic and remedy for rheumatism. Parsley contains Vitamin A, which works with Vitamin E to convert foods to energy, and works against sterility. It also contains amounts of Vitamin C, which stimulates adrenaline and hormones and strengthens the system. Parsley has traces of potassium, also essential to strengthen muscles and glands, and iron which stimulates the blood circulation. In the Middle Ages, the stalks were used to make magic potions to ensnare a loved one, and the roots would also be mixed into a base cream and applied to intimate parts to produce ecstatic results in lovemaking.

ROSEMARY

This popular, pungent culinary herb (Rosmarinus officinalis) is said to improve the memory, and its oil is made into a tonic for digestive, nervous and circulatory problems. The oil is also used to treat hair loss, wind, headaches and arthritis. Rosemary is widely used in savoury recipes such as soups, stews and casseroles, and is particularly good with most meat dishes. It is also used in some dessert preparations, and its long, thin leaves can be dried and powdered or used fresh and whole. In barbecuing, whole clumps of rosemary add flavour to the smoke of the charcoal, imparting its aroma into the cooking meat. Rosemary can be used in a digestive concoction. This intensely aromatic herb was traditionally used in bath water on a daily basis to preserve youth and was widely used in the preparation of scents and perfumes. One of Hungary's queens is said to have invented a potion called 'Hungary Water', an infusion of rosemary tops in spirits or wine. Rosemary is the symbol of friendship, and was carried by bridesmaids at weddings. One herbalist wrote, 'lavender and rosemary is as woman to man', and it was well known as a tonic and stimulant used in magical and possibly sexual rites by the 11th century Welsh Physicians of Myddrai. Mead, a drink common throughout history, contained rosemary, ginger, cloves and lemon rind, infused in fermented honey.

There is a compound in rosemary that replicates a sex hormone, acts on the nervous system and increases the blood circulation, which undoubtedly had an effect on Madame de Sevigne. This 17th century celebrated letter writer who was widowed aged 25 and was subsequently courted throughout France, wrote, "I use rosemary water every day to become inebriated, I always have some handy." One recipe for aphrodisiac rosemary water includes 20g of chopped rosemary leaves, soaked for a week in 12g of anise. The resulting liquid is then drawn off. A teaspoon of this is taken dissolved in a glass of water daily.

RUE

This is an astringent herb, used very frugally in cookery, and is thought to have a beneficial effect on the eyesight. Love potions often contained rue in conjunction with other herbs. Rue (Ruta graveolens) is a blue-green evergreen shrub, and imparts a slightly bitter taste. It is sometimes added to fish or some meat dishes.

SAGE

Sage (Salvia officinalis) is a Southern European plant with wide, bluish-green leaves and widely used in cookery. As it has a very pungent flavour, fresh, powdered or dried sage leaves should be used sparingly. This fragrant herb goes well with any dish, from cheese and fish to meats and poultry. It is commonly used in stuffing, and is used in several sauces. Sage preparations are also used as an antiseptic and anti-inflammatory in cases of sore throats and colds. It is said that preparations containing sage can help make one's wishes come true, and as a result, many ancient magic potions contained sage, not only for this but also for protection from evil forces.

SORREL

Both the leaves and stem of this perennial herb are used in fish, pea or chicken recipes, and sorrel soup is a traditional favourite. Sorrel contains oxalic acid, a substance also found in green bananas, rhubarb and spinach, and it is said to promote sexual interest as it is beneficial to the blood's circulation.

ST JOHN'S WORT

This herb (Hypericum) has been used since ancient times for its restorative effect on the nervous system, and as a remedy for headaches, depression, insomnia and anxiety. St John's Wort is also used in cases of gastritis, stomach ulcers, arthritis, and also to alleviate diarrhoea, as it has both antiseptic and anti-inflammatory properties. St John's Wort is believed to bring happiness to lovers when included in magic spells.

VERBENA

In ancient times, verbena (also known as Vervain, Vervein or Verbane) was dedicated to Venus and, later, women used to wear verbena collars during coitus in order to improve their lover's performance. They even rubbed their bodies with verbena sap. Verbena flowers, soaked in white wine for a week, strained and drunk after a meal, improves the circulation of the blood and increase the reactions.

WORMWOOD

The properties of wormwood were well known to the ancients who concocted many potions containing this herb. The beverage made with this plant is absinthe. Absinthe was invented at the end of the 18th century in France, and became popular as an aphrodisiac drink until it was found that the wormwood oil could cause blindness and insanity. Wormwood can be used to relieve depression and soothe the nerves and can ease the pain of childbirth, and can bring on menstruation. Wormwood can cause dizziness and even convulsions, so it should not be used without the supervision of a qualified herbalist or physician.

Sexy Spices

*"Variety's the very spice of life,
That gives it all its flavour."*
William Cowper (1731-1800)

There are around twenty spices which have aphrodisiac properties, and in the 16th century play by Beaumont and Fletcher, 'Knight of the Burning Pestle', a title full of innuendo, these lines hint at the aphrodisiac qualities of spices.

*"Nose, nose, jolly red nose,
and who gave thee this jolly red nose?
Nutmegs and ginger, cinnamon and cloves
and they gave me this jolly red nose."*

ANISE

These seeds are also known as sweet cumin because anise has a similar aroma. Anise (Pimpinella anisum) is the source of aniseed widely used in cookery. The oval seeds are light brown in colour with a flavour similar to liquorice, due to a volatile essential oil that is used in medicines. Aniseed tea is used in treatments for asthma and bronchitis, and oil of anise is said to be an effective insect repellent, and it is also the active ingredient of the liquor Anisette. The seeds are often used in cooking cakes, bread and desserts. The basis of the stimulant and carminative anise originated in Egypt, where it was burnt with incense in the bed-chambers of the ancient Egyptians.

Early Roman couples would insist on the inclusion of anise in their wedding cakes, and an early Indian lotion for the male suggested the application of a mixture of crushed aniseed and honey. This was said to enlarge the member and give more enjoyment to the female. Aniseed was also chewed to sweeten the breath before sexual encounters. In 18th century France, a highly alcoholic and narcotic liqueur, absinthe, was invented. It was created with an infusion of anise, marjoram, parts of the aromatic elecampane plant and oil of wormwood, and had the accolade of being the aphrodisiac of the 19th century Impressionist painters and French writers. A favourite aphrodisiac of the time comprised of carrots, a classic symbol of fertility, and an aphrodisiac in itself, tossed in butter and fried with anise.

CARAWAY

The aromatic seeds of this plant (Carum carvi) are used in many ways, and the leaves are sometimes used in soups. The seeds are used in baking and to flavour vegetable, meat and fish dishes, as well as soups and pickles. With a flavour similar to that of mint and eucalyptus, the powdered seeds are used to make a tea for digestive disorders. Caraway root is sometimes cooked and eaten as a vegetable. Oil of the caraway is prepared for the treatment of indigestion and to flavour some liqueurs.

Because caraway seed induces the production of milk in lactating females, it is closely associated with the activities of love. Caraway was associated with retention, and was used in love potions to make lovers faithful. It was traditionally offered after a meal to ease digestion, and therefore providing for greater indulgence in love-play. It was commonly chewed to make the breath sweet before love-making, and appears in several recipes for aphrodisiacs, let alone chutneys, pickles, cakes and breads. An aromatic oil made from caraway seeds, blended into a perfume and rubbed onto selected parts of the body, is not only said to be warming but also sexually invigorating. Kummel, a celebrated liqueur, is produced with the addition of the essential oil contained in caraway.

CARDAMOM

Cardamom (Eletteria cardamomum) is a relative of the ginger plant and the seedpods are dried and bleached for use in curries and oriental cooking. A popular spice for cooking desserts and as an ingredient in medicines, the cardamom was thought to be an aphrodisiac. The seeds are used for stimulating the appetite and as cures for indigestion and colic. Perfumes, liqueurs and bitters are also prepared with cardamom. The warming and aromatic seeds have a scented flavour, reminiscent of eucalyptus and its spicy aroma is very sensual.

The book, 'The Perfumed Garden' includes a recipe for an aphrodisiac, which consists of cardamom, cinnamon, ginger, onions and green peas. The Arabs were less inventive and were said to chew cardamom pods, using the spittle as an ointment to excite the male organ. Another love potion suggests the mixing of cardamom seeds with crushed ginger, black pepper and lilac oil. The aphrodisiac qualities of cardamom also feature in 'The Thousand and One Nights', and is referred to as an ingredient of scents, where the oil is used to promote sexual attraction. The seed pod can be used whole or crushed in cooking, but more often the tiny black seeds alone are used either whole or powdered. Cardamom seeds were once known as 'Seeds of Paradise' in their native India, probably because of their stimulating qualities.

CASSIA

This coveted spice comes from bark of a tropical tree (Cinamomum cassia) that is related to cinnamon. The tree itself grows to 10 foot in height. Cassia was recorded as a spice in China as early as 2700BC, and in Egypt in 1550BC. It has the same qualities as cinnamon but, unlike cinnamon, the flavouring of cassia extends into the leaves and flower buds, which are also used in dessert cookery, and its essential oil is sometimes used in treating head colds. Lovers can use cassia or cinnamon to protect their partner from unwanted, lustful attention, so securing their affections.

CHILLIES

Chillies are a well-known aphrodisiac because they warm everything they come into contact with. Not only do chillies warm the body and spirit, but they are also associated with imparting the pain of the 'burn', which in itself can have sexual connotations. However, chillies should be treated with the utmost respect as they can cause excruciating pain if used unwisely! Do not touch sensitive areas, either with chillies, or with hands that have come into contact with chillies! Hot chillies (Capsicum frutescens) are native to the Americas, as opposed to the peppercorn, which is the fruit of a vine from India. The chilli plant can reach two metres tall, and there are around 100 varieties.

The many shapes, sizes and colours of chillies range from the fiery-hot scotch bonnet, which can be yellow, orange or red, to the Poblano, which is black-green in colour. There are many other chillies – the jalapeno, which is dark green, the Mulatto which is dark brown with a wrinkled skin, and the small, bright green Serrano chilli. The mild Anaheim chilli is red or green, and the Pasilla is long, thin and dark. The small, lantern-shaped, orange-red Habanero chilli is the hottest of all. There is also the very hot bird eye chilli, and the cayenne chilli – both long, thin and red.

The bright Guajillo chilli is used for colouring food and imparting a delightful warm heat. The mild Ancho chilli is also commonly used dried for cooking sauce, like the Romesco. Other chillies more commonly dried include Cascabel, Chipotle, Guajillo and Pasilla. Several varieties of chilli are dried and ground to make cayenne pepper. The Guindilla, Morron and Nora varieties are more commonly dried. Dried red chillies are ground to make chilli pepper and some are steeped in vegetable oil to create a pungent cooking oil.

Chillies are also used medicinally as a stimulant, an aid to digestion and to produce warmth. Tabasco sauce, named after a place and river in Mexico, is made from the pickled flesh of chillies and can be extremely hot, coming in a variety of forms; Habanero sauce, or salsa, being the hottest one made from singularly hot chilli. The word salsa was first used in a commercial musical in 1928.

CINNAMON

Cinnamon (Cinnamomum zeylanicum) comes from the bark of a 50 foot tree, which is stunted to eight foot when cultivated. The thin bark is stripped from the trunk and dried to form quills which are powdered, used whole mainly in dessert cookery, or mixed with other spices. Thought to be an aphrodisiac, this ancient spice has an essential oil that is both astringent and antiseptic. It is used to aid digestion, and in the treatment of stomach disorders. This is one of the oldest spices known to man, and has been written about in Chinese herbals since 2500BC. In the Bible, there is a reference to prostitutes using cinnamon, together with aloes and myrrh, as an aphrodisiac perfume. Its oil was known to be an ingredient of the sacred oil used in the tabernacle. One of the ancient Four Officinal Capitals, or Classical remedies and aphrodisiacs set down over two thousand years ago, 'Doscordium', contained cinnamon, gentian, germander, ginger, honey, opium and sorrel.

Cinnamon was also one of the eight ingredients in 'Carmelite Water'. Cinnamon has an elusive aroma, and was well known as an accompaniment to chocolate (in itself a sexual stimulant) as a recipe for a traditional love potion. One early description of the growing cinnamon tree, which can reach heights of fifty feet, is sexually evocative and reflects the aphrodisiac applications of this pungent spice. The cinnamon has "numerous flowers, borne in lax panicles on long pubescent peduncles." It is interesting to note that the word 'peduncle' also means the 'stalklike process in the animal body'. Cinnamon has an essential oil, which is the active aphrodisiac ingredient of this spice. In India, cinnamon was mixed with ginger, cardamom, onions and peas to create an aphrodisiac potion. Cinnamon was also used in Chinese love potions and philtres, and the Arab pharmacists recommended a mixture of cinnamon, onions, cardamom and ginger as the ultimate aphrodisiac.

CLOVES

Initially, Arab traders encouraged the propogation of cloves in Zanzibar, then the Dutch held a monopoly on cloves (Eygenia caryophyllus) until the end of the 18th century. After which, the French began propogating the 40 foot high evergreen tree, of which cloves are the dried buds, on their colonies of Mauritius in the Indian Ocean, and Cayenne in South America. The name comes from the Latin for nail, 'clavus' as the buds resemble a nail. Cloves are used in a multitude of culinary recipes, both in savoury and sweet cookery, and contain powerful and volatile antiseptic oil. Cloves are also an ingredient in perfumes and soaps, and the oil is used to relieve toothache, aid digestion and stop diarrhoea.

Cloves were used in China and India to sweeten the breath before love-making, a practice known as far back as the 3rd century BC. The ancient Persians were known to have used cloves in love potions, and they are still an ingredient of scents and perfumes today. It is the pungency of the cloves' volatile oil, distilled from the buds, stalks and leaves that imparts flavour to both savoury and sweet recipes alike; making them seductively warm to the taste. Up until the 14th century, mead was a popular drink, considered an aphrodisiac and made from fermented honey with cloves, ginger, rosemary and lemon rind. It is said that four robbers used a special preparation when plundering graves during an outbreak of the plague in Europe during the 17th century. This unguent, known as the 'Vinegar of the Four Thieves', could well have doubled as an aphrodisiac perfume, as it consisted of cloves, lavender, marjoram, rosemary and vinegar.

CORIANDER

Coriander (Coriandrum sativum) has been known in culinary and medicinal circles for thousands of years. It belongs to the chervil, cumin and dill family, and has jagged feathery leaves. It is the leaves that are used extensively in cookery, both as a decoration in salads and as flavouring. The ripened seeds are dried and used crushed in both savoury and dessert cookery as an aromatic and fragrant spice. Coriander seeds are also a major ingredient in curry powder, and in the production of a number of sauces and marinades. Coriander also has digestive properties and was thought to be an aphrodisiac. This is one of the earliest herbs known to have been used by man. The Greek physician, Hippocrates, recommended coriander as a stimulant for the system and, before that, it was mentioned in Sanskrit and early papyrus writings. In 1611, Carmelite monks devised a potion containing coriander seed, lemon peel, balm, nutmeg, cinnamon, angelica, cloves and wine. The seeds are also used in another ancient love potion which involves an invocation whilst grinding seven seeds and infusing them in spring water. Coriander seeds were also one of the eight ingredients of the 17th century preparation 'Carmelite Water'. Both the seeds and the leaves are used in preparing warming, fragrant and stimulating dishes, including curries, soups and meat. Platine de Cremone recommended that coriander seeds be soaked in wine to create an euphoric effect in women.

CUBEBS

The small berries of this little perennial climber (Piper cubeba) when dried and ground can be substituted for black pepper. The shrub originated in Java, and resembles allspice in taste and aroma. The pungent fruit of the plant belongs to the Indian pepper family. In rural areas medicinal tobacco is made from the berry, which also has culinary uses. The Arabs were known to make a poultice of the crushed spice, which is spread on the male organ to stimulate pleasure in both the male and female.

CUMIN

The seeds of this small plant (Cuminum cyminum) are particularly pungent, aromatic and warming, and were used for their ability to aid digestion as well as flavouring foods in pickles, chutneys, rice and vegetable dishes. It is also used in many Middle Eastern recipes, and to flavour some liqueurs. Oil is extracted from the seed, which is also used in perfumes. Some believe that cumin has the power to ensure the fidelity of one's partner.

FRANKINCENSE

This ancient plant (Boswellia thurifera) is used to make a fragrant oil, which has both antiseptic and anti-inflammatory properties. Frankincense has been known to have aphrodisiac powers for centuries. Toiletries made from frankincense are said to preserve the complexion, and the astringent oil relieves anxiety and stress, and thus promotes lovemaking.

GINGER

Ginger (Zingiber officinale) is a native to Asia, and it is the root of a perennial plant. The tuber has a light brown skin and contains a firm, aromatic and pungent flesh that is used either chopped or ground as a spice. Although ginger originates in Asia, it is widely grown in Africa and China, and there is a Caribbean version native to Jamaica. Ginger is widely used in cooking world wide, in marinades, sauces, soups, drinks and even ice cream.

The root of ginger is used both in sweet and savoury dishes, and medicinally it aids digestion, restores circulation and is said to be an aphrodisiac. Ginger is widely used in chutneys and pickles and is also crystallised as a dessert.

As an aphrodisiac, ginger can be taken internally in foods, drinks and potions, or applied externally as in one male ointment which includes honey, lilac oil and the pungent irritant pellitory root. Ginger is used in numerous recipes, and induces a warm, amatory feeling. One early Arabic aphrodisiac consists of ginger, sesame seeds, lavender, cloves and nutmeg. Yet another love potion consists of crushed ginger, cardamom seeds, black pepper and lilac oil. Ginger was also an ingredient in one of the ancient Four Officinal Capitals, or Classical remedies and aphrodisiacs proposed over 2000 years ago. This was known as 'Dioscordium', which contained ginger, cinnamon, gentian, germander, honey, opium and sorrel. It was also common to infuse a concoction of cream and milk with the pungent aroma of ginger, by boiling them together with sugar and powdered ginger. Jerome Cardan, the 16th century physician, wrote that ginger "helps a lustful nature".

MUSTARD

This ancient spice (Brassica nigra, black mustard and Brassica alba, white mustard) is often eaten with cress as seeds or ground to make mustard powder. Mustard is widely used in meat dishes, with cheese and as a pungent additive to sauces. Its warming qualities are used in treating respiratory disorders and in the kitchen mustard is widely used in pastes consisting of vinegar, sugar, herbs and mustard powder. There are numerous forms of mustard, both in paste and powder, which have many uses in the kitchen.

In ancient times, to make a paste for stimulating the sexual glands, ground mustard seeds were mixed with verjuice or grape must. This preparation was known as 'ardent must', which in the 12th century became 'mustard'. A mixture of ground mustard, mustard oil, rosemary and honey was sometimes rubbed on the skin of the male member. This application tended to sting, but it also dilated the blood vessels and therefore increased the circulation, improving the erection. A French preparation, Moutarde a la ravigote, known as the 'reviver', contains mustard, chillies and ginger – beware!

NUTMEG

The nutmeg is the seed of a fruit native to the Mollucca Islands of Indonesia. Nutmeg (Mysterica frangans) is the brownish, pungent, egg-shaped seed of the tree. The seed is surrounded by a lacy red membrane, which is known as mace. The yellow fruit surrounding the seed is discarded when harvesting. Both are ground to make the spices nutmeg and mace. Nutmeg was used widely by the ancients of the Orient in a blend of nutmeg, sesame, lavender, ginger and cloves. A particularly volatile offering relies on the amphetamines contained in the spice. When mixed with the bromocriptine contained in avocado, the methylenedioxyamphetamine in nutmeg produces a potent male sexual stimulant. Nutmeg was also one of the seven herbal ingredients in 'Carmelite Water', and is used to stimulate the circulation, essential in sexual activity. Ground nutmeg is also used in drinks, savoury and sweet dishes. Up until Victorian times, people would carry a nutmeg with them in decorative silver cases to sprinkle on foods and drinks. Mace, the lacy, brilliant scarlet covering of the nutmeg is also a valued spice. It was traditionally given, along with nutmeg, to medieval bridegrooms before their wedding nights to increase their ardour. Nutmeg and mace were boiled together with honey, eggs and a lavish measure of fortified wine and was drunk before venturing into the nuptial bedchamber.

PEPPER

The Indian peppercorn vine (Piper nigram) is the source of many types of cooking pepper. The dried, unripe fruit are ground to produce black pepper, and when they ripen they turn red and can be shelled and ground to produce white pepper. Pepper acts as a cooling agent, settling the stomach while stimulating the appetite. In Classical times, a favoured love potion included pepper ground together with savory, mushrooms and nettle seeds. Another included crushed black peppercorns, cardamom seeds, crushed ginger and lilac oil. In the Southern states of America, a traditional love charm said to induce unbounded desire in women was the root of St John's Wort, dipped in pepper and sugar, and placed under the subject's bed. However, it had to be the plant with a small root, as that with a long root was sacrosanct to men and known as High John the Conqueror, whilst the small root was said to stimulate women and referred to as 'Little John'! Pepper was also an essential ingredient in another traditional male balm, said to be a powerful aphrodisiac when applied to the male member. This lotion consisted of a mixture of white thorn apple, a known hallucinogen, honey and freshly ground black peppercorns.

SAFFRON

The orange-red styles or stamens are collected from the saffron crocus (Crocus stavius), and are dried to make this powerful colouring agent, used particularly in rice dishes and paellas. As the styles must be picked by hand, this is the most expensive spice, almost equalling the price of gold in weight, with a very delicate flavour but powerful as a colouring agent. Saffron has long been associated with aphrodisiacs in the Orient, as it is known to have restorative and strengthening qualities. Saffron was also one of the four ingredients of the Classical 'Capitals', known as 'Philonium'. Francis Bacon, in the early 17th century, wrote "the English are rendered sprightly by a liberal use of saffron in sweetmeats and broths." It was also said by the 17th century diarist, John Aubrey, that Cornish girls would add some of their pubic hair to their traditional saffron cakes or breads, to heighten the ardour of their lovers. He called this 'cockle bread', a "relique of naturall magick, and unlawful philtrum." The sexual connotations of the intense yellow colour produced from saffron was widespread, as it was the traditional wear of nymphs in ancinet times. Maybe in recollection of this practice, the prostitutes of Dodge City in the days of the Wild West, were made to wear yellow to indicate their profession. Saffron is said to have the same effect as hormones and stimulates the erogenous zones.

SESAME

The oil rich sesame plant (Sesamum indicum) originated in Africa where it was called Benne. The oil extracted from the tiny seeds of the five-foot high plant is used as cooking oil as well as medicinally for its laxative qualities. The seeds are generally white, or a creamy colour. Sesame contains quantities of iron, which is good for the blood and is an excellent source of protein. The zinc contained in the seeds promotes the health of the male organs and is essential for the potency of sperm. Sesame seeds are a symbol of fertility, and an old Arab aphrodisiac recipe consists of sesame, lavender, ginger, cloves and nutmeg.

VANILLA

Of more than 17,000 varieties of orchids, vanilla (Vanilla fragrans) is the only one which produces an exotic perfume from both its pod and bean. The vine can grow to 15 metres and thrives in tropical lowland forest. Originating in Mexico, vanilla (or tlilxochitl) was the ancient Aztecs favourite additive to cocoa, chocolate or xocoatl, which gave their drink a musky flavour tempered with chilli. The

Spanish conquistador, Bernal Diaz, who accompanied Henando Cortez to Mexico in the early 16th century, reported that Montezuma consumed vast quantities of this beverage. The name vanilla, from the word vaina or pod, which is incidentally the same etymological stem of the word 'vagina'.

The long, green pods remain on the plant for six to nine months before being picked. They are harvested before the seed-bearing pods are ripe. The pod, or bean, has to be cured to release its pungent odour, by steeping it in boiling water when green and about seven inches long. The pods are then sweated in cloth, matured and oven dried slowly over several weeks until white crystals appear on the pod's now deep brown surface. Vanilla has a long-standing reputation as an aphrodisiac; the Aztecs of early Mexico mixed this spice with cocoa to produce a stimulating aphrodisiac, and it was a potency-inducing spice in Victorian times. Vanilla oil was also used in the preparation of early love perfumes.

For a pleasurable dip, which may lead to amorous activity, share a bowl of quarter of a pound of pure chocolate, melted over a low heat with a teaspoon of grated vanilla pod, and two whole vanilla pods. When hot, add two tablespoons of honey. Alternatively, share a bath into which four drops of vanilla essence have been added.

The Fruits of Love

"Of Man's First Disobedience, and the Fruit
Of that Forbidden Tree…"
John Milton (1608-1674)

APPLE

The apple is one of the earliest examples of a food being presented
as an icon of love. The apple was one of man's first foods, and represented fertility. In Classical times, and before, the apple was the
accepted symbol of sexual seduction. To the ancients, it embodied
the ultimate aphrodisiac. By Medieval times, aphrodisiacs were
regarded as sinful and 'forbidden fruit'. Therefore, when translators of
the Bible came across the object that Eve proffered to Adam, they
opted for the image of an apple.

We have already seen how widely the image of an apple was used
throughout history to symbolise the aphrodisiac and how a range of
fruit acquired the name Love Apple. We have also seen how the
Greeks and Romans evolved whole cultures around sexual stimulation, and even lent the name of one of their gods to the science,
aphrodisia. Later, we looked at how a wide range of different stimulants to the senses can lead the mind to release the essential hormones needed to induce, sustain and complete the act of coitus.

Throughout nature, there is a great selection of fruits, nuts, vegetables, plants, herbs and spices that have been found to have varying aphrodisiac qualities. Some contain substances that can stimulate the body sexually, and others may induce sexual interest with their aroma, shape or texture.

BANANAS

Bananas (Musa sapientum) not only have sexual connotations due to their phallic shape, but their skin contains the aphrodisiac alkaloid, bufotenine. This hallucinogen can be obtained by baking the banana and scraping out the insides of the skins. There are more than 300 different varieties of banana, from bright yellow to red, and from the length of a finger to over a foot in length. Bananas contain high levels of potassium and carbohydrates, are rich in Vitamin C and low in protein and fat. Bananas contain 94 calories per 100g of fruit. The dark purple petals of the male flower can be peeled away to reveal the edible 'heart', which can be included in salads. They can also be cooked in boiling water for 20 minutes, when the outer purple petals are discarded and the centre eaten like artichoke leaves.

BETEL NUT

The betel nut palm grows in India and the Pacific, and the powdered nut is widely used throughout Asia. Arecoline is an alkaline and volatile oil found in the betel nut that is believed to possess aphrodisiac qualities. This oil speeds up respiration, stimulates energy, gives a sense of euphoria and decreases pressure on the heart. Betel nut is usually chewed together with burnt lime (which releases the oil) and added nutmeg, cardamom or turmeric.

CHOCOLATE

"To a coffee-house to drink jocolatte, very good!"
Diary of Samuel Pepys, 1664

It is thought that the cocoa tree originated in the river basin of the Orinoco, and was first used by the Amerindians around 4000 years ago. So valued was the bean, that the ancient Aztecs of Mexico once used the beans from the tree they knew as Nahuatl caca for their currency, hence the saying 'money growing on trees!'

Around 100 cocoa beans would buy a slave in the kingdom of the Aztecs prior to the arrival of the Europeans, with Hernando Cortez' first expedition into Mexico in 1519. They found that the local Aztecs and Mayas processed the beans in much the same way as it is done now. They roasted the beans, ground them, winnowed the shells from the kernel and ground the nibs on stone tables known as metapes. The powder resulting was known as chocolatle, from which we get the word chocolate.

Powdered cocoa beans were also whisked into a drink, mixed with vanilla and other spices. The Aztecs prepared the bitter, spicy drink with a special wooden whisk, which turned the mixture almost solid with the consistency of honey. This cold preparation was said to dissolve in the mouth. The Emperor of Mexico, Montezuma, was known to drink 50 cups of the beverage known as 'xocoatl' every day, which he spooned from a gold chalice with a finely wrought gold spoon.

Cocoa as a drink, was first introduced to Europe via Spain, where the idea of sweetening it with sugar and heating it evolved. The Spanish jealously guarded their recipe for chocolate for over a hundred years. In their ignorance, when the English, Dutch and French captured Spanish ships carrying cargoes of cacao, they dumped the lot over the side! The first chocolate drinking house opened in London in 1657, and competed with the traditional coffee houses. By the 1700's, cocoa became a popular drink in many of the coffee houses in London. The Quakers extolled the virtues of cocoa over the evils of gin, stating that it would 'clear the head, and drive away alcoholic vapours'. However, most of the cocoa houses recommended recipes which included brandy, sherry or wine. One such recipe comprised of chocolate, sugar, egg yolks and claret, whisked to a frothy consistency.

In 1705, the Dutch doctor, Stephani Blancardi, wrote this about the first cup of chocolate which he tasted. "It is a veritable balm of the mouth, for the maintaining of all glands and humours in a good state of health. Thus it is, that all who do drink it possess a sweet breath." By the late 1840's, cocoa powder was being mixed with sugar and cocoa butter to make a paste which became the first eating chocolate. The first eating chocolate was produced in England in 1847. In England, cocoa remained an expensive commodity until 1853, when the English Prime Minister Gladstone reduced the import duty on the product. Meanwhile, in Switzerland in 1875, a machine was invented which added condensed milk to the eating chocolate paste, and produced the first solid milk chocolate. The Swiss are still the largest consumers of chocolate per head in the world, eating an average 22 pounds each a year! The earliest commercial attempt at growing cacao in West Africa, now the world's leading source, was in 1879 when the first beans were planted in Ghana.

"Persons who drink chocolate regularly are conspicuous for unfailing health and immunity from the host of minor ailments which mar the enjoyment of life; they are also less inclined to lose weight."
'The Philosopher in the Kitchen', Brillat-Savarin (1755-1825)

The French gastronomist, Brillat-Savarin, in his 'Physiology of Taste', also recommends that the best way to prepare chocolate was with the additions of vanilla and cinnamon, and made a broth to restore his manhood from carrots, onions, parsley, sugar, chocolate and ambergris. Mrs Hannah Glasse, the author of a famed cookery book, also suggested the addition of "three grains of musk, and as much ambergrease". Ambergris, a product of the sperm whale, is a tried and tested aphrodisiac used by King Louis XV's lover, Madame du Barry, and Madame de Pompadour. Madame du Barry fed chocolate to her lovers, and Casanova and the Marquis de Sade both favoured chocolate as an aphrodisiac. In the 18th century, one expert claimed that his wife had given birth to three sets of twins after indulging in copious amounts of chocolate! In the early days, cooks also experimented by adding such ingredients as aniseed, ginger and even pepper, yet three more aphrodisiacs! In 1941, Milton Hershey's chocolate company began production of a 600-calorie 'survival bar' to supply the American armed forces in the Second World War. Around the same time, a Forrest Mars began making his familiar chocolate Mars bars.

Chocolate is rich in Vitamins B and D, calcium, magnesium and contains the stimulant caffeine. It also contains four per cent protein, carbohydrates and 31 per cent fat, and is one of the richest sources of iron. It is used medically in the treatment of kidney disorders and high blood pressure. Because chocolate also contains small amounts of the amphetamine-like phenylethylamine, a chemical produced in the brain during amorous activity, it is suggested

that chocolate can be an effective aphrodisiac. It also contains theobromine, a recognised stimulant, from which it derives its Latin
name, Theobroma cacao. The theobromine in chocolate is said to
increase alertness. Chocolate also contains 500 calories per 100g in
weight, and is rich in an antioxidant called phenol, which is said to
reduce congestion in arteries.

"Twill make Old Women Young and Fresh,
Create a New Motion of the Flesh,
And cause them long for you know what,
If they but taste of chocolate."
James Wadsworth

COCONUT

The coconut (Cocos nucifera) has long been ascribed aphrodisiac
qualities. It has crossed the world naturally on sea currents and taken
root in just about every tropical shore. The tree, which is really a
palm, is originally indigenous to Pacific Polynesia and has been cultivated for over 200 years. The feathery, leafy crown produces the
famous nut, and its leaves can grow to 20 foot in length. Thatching,
baskets and brooms are made from the fronds and the husk is used to
make coir, from which matting is made. The kernel has a hard shell
used in the manufacture of charcoal and utensils.

When young and green, the coconut contains a refreshing milk and jelly-like meat. When mature, the jelly turns to a delicious white meat, used dried to make copra, from which oil is extracted and soap is produced from the desiccated meat.

Whilst the kernel is maturing, its hollow inside produces a useful white flesh, or meat, and a sweet milk builds up inside. The milk contains just 18 calories per 100g, and the immature meat contains 122 calories per 100g, whilst the calorific value of the mature nut is among the highest in the plant world, at 296 per 100g of meat. The milk of the coconut is often mixed with rum to create the delicious 'sahoco' drink. Coconuts are a fine source of iron and phosphorous. Cooking oil, coconut cream and coconut meat are also made from the nut, which is used to make margarine, soaps, suntan lotions and confectionery. Coconut is also used in numerous sauces, particularly marinades, often combined with lime.

The coconut is the source of many cooking ingredients. In the Pacific, where the coconut originated, its milk was mixed with the Fijian Kava kava, to make a narcotic aphrodisiac. In India, the coconut was dedicated to the goddess of fertility and was prominent at weddings for the obvious reasons. One Oriental aphrodisiac recipe includes coconut cream, carrots, milk, brown sugar, cardamoms, butter and almonds.

COLA NUT

The Cola Nut tree, a native of West Africa, is a source of a herbal type of cocaine, and different from the Coca plant which only grows in the high mountains of South America, and produces the drug. The nut of the Cola tree (Cola nitida) or kola, is the source of the secret ingredient of the Cola drink. In South America it is widely used as a stimulant, a hunger suppressant and an aphrodisiac. The nut of this tree is usually chewed and it contains three per cent caffeine.

DAMIANA

This shrub, which grows in the southern part of the US and Mexico, has a Latin name which announces its aphrodisiac qualities, Turnera aphrodisiaca. For many centuries, the women of Mexico infused the oval leaves of Damiana in boiling water, to create an aphrodisiac. They also took it with the local liqueur, tequila, two hours before making love, in order to vastly improve their enjoyment. The drug, damianian, produces euphoric feelings and stimulates the sexual organs.

DITA

This tall tropical tree, also called Alstonia, grows in India and South East Asia, and its seeds have long been known to have aphrodisiac qualities. The tree's bark was once used as a parchment, hence its

Latin name, Alstonia scholaris. Although the bark and seeds are used in making a tea to cure dysentery and diarrhoea, it is the alkaloid allergin – chlorogenic acid – contained in the seeds that is the active aphrodisiac. A preparation made by soaking the seeds in water, produces genital erotic tinglings, prolongs erection and delays orgasm.

GUARANA

This South American nut has the highest caffeine content of any nut and it is correspondingly a powerful stimulant. The three-celled fruit contains a flesh-coloured seed like a horse chestnut, that must be roasted for six hours before use. It was traditionally used as a medicine by the Amerindians to cure headaches, neuralgia and nervous complaints and it is now used in a number of so-called 'smart drinks' in the West. The nut is an appetite suppressant but the oil which they contain, guarnine, is an effective aphrodisiac as it sharpens the mind and slows the pulse rate. An ancient Arawak recipe that is designed to suppress hunger, is a mixture of ground Guarana nut with cassava flour making a sweet culinary paste known as 'pasta guarana'.

LIGNUM VITAE

The resin and bark of the Lignum Vitae, or Tree of Life, has medicinal properties and has also long been regarded as an aphrodisiac. It was also known in the early days as the natural 'penicillin'. The bark is used as a cathartic, the blue flowers as a laxative and the fruit is edible, and an excellent source of revitalisation for the male.

MANGO

The Mango (Mangifera indica) is a common ingredient in many chutneys, pickles, sauces and marinades and imparts a truly tropical, fruity taste to food. Mangoes are now widespread throughout the tropics although they are indigenous to Asia. Mango trees are ever-green, tall, with shiny leaves and a hardwood trunk favoured by carvers and furniture-makers. Mangoes are a sweet-tart, juicy fruit and can vary in weight from plum-size to mangoes weighing two or more pounds. They are generally heart or kidney-shaped, green when unripe and range in colour when ripe from red or yellow, to cream and green. Mangoes contain 10 to 20 per cent sugar, and are rich in carotene, Vitamins A, B and C. They also contain traces of potassium and other mineral traces. The flesh is usually a deep orange colour and fibrous, attached to a large, flat centre seed. The skin should give when pressed, indicating its ripeness.

Mango eating can be such a messy, yet sexy experience, that some people recommend eating mangoes in the bath! To prepare mangoes as neatly and cleanly as possible, remove the flesh from the large, flat seed. A sharp knife should be inserted into the side until the seed is felt. The knife-point should be eased around the circumference of the fruit, edging in, so that one half of the fruit is separated from the seed. To prepare mangoes as an attractive dish, score lines through the flesh down to the skin, about a centimetre wide, vertically and then horizontally. Then invert the intact skin into a concave shape, and the diced flesh should stand proud of the skin in a dome shape.

MATE

The leaves of this South American fruit tree, mate (Ilex paraguyensis) contain up to three per cent caffeine and they have long been used as an aphrodisiac. The revolutionary icon, Che Guevara, swore by mate before having sex.

PAPAYA

The Papaya (Carica papaya), or Paw Paw, is also known as 'fruta bomba' in some areas, as the word 'papaya' is local slang for an intimate part of the female anatomy. When cut in half, the fruit resembles this organ and its rich musky aroma has sexual overtones. It name, papaya, comes from the Arawak Amerindian name 'ababai'. The succulent, large, greenish fruit has a delicious orange to pink flesh around a mass of black seeds, and these seeds have long been used in contraceptive potions. They are also used in preparations to treat constipation. The fruit grows on a tree, which is really a large herb, growing to around 20 foot in height. Both the fruit and leaves sprout from the top of a long, thin, grey-coloured naked trunk, marked with leaf scars. On the top of the tall trunk is a 'topknot' of decorative shiny green leaves. The flowers can be male, female or both sexes, many of which fall to leave just enough male flowers to pollinate the remaining females.

When the fruit appears, it grows in clusters, spiralling down close to the smooth grey trunk. A native of the Caribbean, the fruit ripens all year round, and can weigh between 400g to several kilos. The papaya tree's fruit is rich in vitamins and contains an enzyme, papain, which breaks down protein. The papaya is used as a meat tenderiser, and a derivative of papain – papaverin – is used as a painkiller. Papaverin is also used in contraceptive pills and as an aphrodisiac. Other properties in the leaves and bark of the tree are used in medicines. The enzyme of the papaya is also used in chewing gum, and in the manufacture of moisturising cream. When young and green, the fruit can be treated as a vegetable, with a taste resembling courgettes. It is most commonly eaten raw, and a touch of lime or lemon juice brings out the fruit's delicate flavour. Unripe, it can be used in chutneys, soups and stews, and is said to be good for high blood pressure.

When yellow streaks appear on the papaya fruit's skin, it is ready to be harvested and the addition of lime juice and ground ginger can enhance its flavour. Papaya is a good source of Vitamin C, and contains some iron. The papaya is low in calorific value, containing just 28 calories per 100g. The deep-lobed leaves, which also contain the enzyme papain, can be wrapped around meat and boiled to tenderise it. When dried, these leaves can be substituted for tobacco.

PASSION FRUIT

The passion in this fruit's name unfortunately does not refer to sexual passion, although the fruit is said to have aphrodisiac qualities, and is the basis of the drink Parfait d'Amour, or 'Perfect Love'. The passion fruit's cousin, the giant granadilla, is the source of the South American aphrodisiac liqueur, Maracuja. When Spanish missionaries arrived in the New World of the 16th century, they found a remarkable vine that produced a curious and beautiful purple, gold and white flower, but an ugly looking fruit. The flower's petals and stamens reminded the missionaries of Christ's Crown of Thorns, the Five Wounds of Saviour and the Cross' Three Nails. Thus, they named the plant the Passion flower, (Passiflora edulis).

The fruit of the passion vine is disappointingly brown-purple and wrinkled, but has a glorious, acidy-sweet taste. The hard pithy skin is discarded but the entire contents can be eaten raw, or used to flavour desserts, served with other fruits to bring out their flavour or to make a drink.

PLANTAIN

Varieties of the banana include the Plantain (Musa paradisaica), a vegetable type of the common banana, of which there are many different types. Plantain, often known as Adam's Fig, are less sweet than bananas, with a higher starch content and are larger than the familiar yellow bananas. Plantain can be boiled, fried or baked and used as a vegetable or dessert, depending how ripe they are. Both bananas and plantain are high in energy and fibre, and contain potassium, folic acid and minerals, which add to their aphrodisiac qualities. They also contain Vitamin B, some iron and calcium, and are said to prevent gastric ulcers. Plantain contains more calories than bananas, with 122 per 10g of fruit.

POMEGRANATE

Pomegranates have long been a symbol of fertility, especially in Indian and Chinese cultures, and silver pommels in the shape of pomegranates appear in many cultures, not least on the wooden handles of the Scrolls of the Judaic Law in every synagogue. This symbol of Judaism pre-dates the Star of David by centuries. Pomegranates (Punica granatum) grow on a small deciduous tree, with bright orange-red flowers. The fruit are round and hard-skinned, ranging from pale pink to red. Inside the bitter pith, the fruit consists of numerous fleshy cells or juice sacs, known as arils, containing tiny edible seeds, which is why the Spanish have given it the name

Granada, their word for grenade. The pomegranate, Maracuya and the Granadilla are all members of the Passion fruit family. Native to the Americas, they mature on the vine throughout the year, reaching around 100g in weight, and are rich in Vitamin C. Pomegranates are made into a liqueur, Grenadine, used as a flavouring in ice cream and as a juice for cooking. The indelible dye of the juice was used to colour Persian carpets.

The Virile Vegetable

"Erection is chiefly caused by parsnips, artichokes, turnips, candied ginger, and crushed acorns in sweet white wine."
Aristotle (385-322 BC)

Probably the most intimate aphrodisiac is that which is consumed by the mouth, an apt analogy for the sexual act. Many vegetables, particularly root vegetables, have a long history of sexual association, not only because of their shape, but because they are a food which often contains aphrodisiac or stimulant properties.

ARTICHOKE

The 16th century herbalist, John Gerard, extolled the virtues of the Jerusalem artichoke, stating "This middle pulp when boiled with the broth of fat flesh with pepper added makes a dainty dish being pleasant to the taste and accounted good to produce bodily desire. It stayeth the involuntary course of the natural seed."

ASPARAGUS

Ultra-phallic in shape, the white spears of asparagus strike up through the ground with their purple tips being the buds of the fernlike plant, which is cut well before the fronds open. Long and plump, the asparagus has a bulbous tip which is the most tender part of the shaft. The ancient Egyptians, Greeks, Romans and Moors all recognised the potent shape of the asparagus, and endowed it with aphrodisiac qualities because of this. In 'The Perfumed Garden', it was recommended to boil asparagus, then fry it in fat, egg yolk and condiments to ensure an erotic effect. John Gerard went further. He recommended that the young buds he steeped in wine before eating to "stir up the lust of the body". The great herbalist Nicolas Culpeper suggests that "a decoration of the roots being taken fasting several mornings together, stirreth up bodily lust in man and woman." Usually, the shoots are boiled and dipped in melted butter, then sucked, rather than bitten. Few vegetables are eaten in such a seductive way.

BEANS

Much has been written about the virile qualities of protein-rich pulses, even though beans have a notorious side effect. Beans have long been associated with the continuity of life, and a symbol of virility. In 'The Perfumed Garden', it is suggested that a potent concoction made from green peas boiled with onions, cinnamon, ginger and cardamom, "create for the consumer amorous passion and strength for coitus." The word 'bean-feast' comes from the ancient association of the bean with fertility, and it was recommended to walk your lover through a field of beans to ensure that he or she would submit to your amorous advances. An Arabic story tells of Abu el Heidja, who ate a quantity of chickpeas with honey and camel's milk, before deflowering eighty virgins in one night!

CAPERS

These are the mottled, greenish-brown unopened buds of the shrub (Capparis spinosa), usually pickled in vinegar. Capers are used as a pickle and their warm, strong, spicy flavour makes them an ideal additive to a number of sauces. The spicy tang of capers is said to bring on amorous sensations.

CARROTS

This herbaceous plant, with its large edible root, is widely used in the preparation of sauces and dips, as well as soups and stews. The most common carrot is the bright orange variety, although there are white and purple carrots. Their size and shape also varies considerably. Carrots contain a large amount of Vitamin C and quantities of sugar. Sweet and fresh, they also contain amounts of Vitamin A and B and iron, and are known to restore the nervous system. Carrots are also known to assist in mentally promoting sexual activity, and this is probably why the ancient Greeks called them 'philion', their word for loving, and used them as an aphrodisiac. Since Classical times, and probably before, the carrot was domestically cultivated in its native Afghanistan, and they were mashed and mixed with cardamom to create an elixir served before love-making. Another favourite aphrodisiac comprised of carrots tossed in butter and fried with anise.

In 1542, the physician Andrew Boorde wrote that carrots "increase nature", in his famous 'Dyetary'.

CASSAVA

The Cassava is just one of a vast range of around 160 varieties of tuber which grow naturally in its native soil in the Caribbean and South America. Most widely used of these are cassava, yucca, manioc or malanga (like a sweet potato), boniato, taro and more than 600 varieties of yam. Of the two main varieties of cassava used in cookery, one is faintly sweet and the other rather bitter. The juice extracted from the bitter variety is called cassareep, and is used as an ingredient of some sauces. The cassava tuber grows underground and has a tall, thin, knobbly stalk sprouting in a flush of wide, bright green leaves. The shrub can grow to seven foot high, and it is propagated by planting sections of the stem. Harvesting the tubers can begin eight months to two years after planting. The cassava is an indigenous plant to the Americans, and is a large, brown tuber with a rough skin and a firm white flesh. The ground flesh can be used to make a flour, or as a soup additive. It can also be boiled or roasted and used as a vegetable. The leaves of the cassava are also edible and are usually boiled.

Cassava is the source of tapioca and arrowroot, and is high in starch, antioxidants and low in protein. Cassava also produces a chemical, linamarin, and the enzyme linamarase, which breaks down the lina-marin into the cyanide compound which is washed out of the ground flesh before the cassava is eaten. The gene which produces the linamarase is now known to eradicate cancerous tumours. The high starch content of cassava flour, used in stiffening soups, is also held to endow the male member with similar qualities.

CELERY

Celery has long been the butt of jokes with sexual innuendoes, related to its long stem and supposed bedroom antics involving wet celery sticks. Apart from this, celery is a vegetable that has many uses, both hot and cold.

Celery seeds are used in tomato juice and seafood dishes, pickles, chutneys, soups and stews. A sleep-promoting tea can be made from the seeds, and a tonic for rheumatism is prepared from an infusion of celery seeds. The juice of celery also has a Vitamin A and C content, as well as traces of calcium, manganese, sulphur, potassium and organic sodium. The plant contains an essential oil used to flavour a salt-based seasoning. Preparations from the oil are used in treatments for asthma, bronchitis, liver diseases and fevers. The leaves and stalk are also used as a vegetable, both cooked and uncooked. The long stalks of celery might have played a jocular role in sexual practices, but are actually the source of a mild aphrodisiac.

Celery, like celeriac and truffles, contains pig pheromones, subconsciously detected by the olfactory nerves and similar to those exuded by humans. These pheromones are responsible for attraction in male and female alike, which is probably why celery soup is so popular! Grimod de la Reyniere said of celery "...our conscience obliges us to warn shy people (from it), that they might abstain from it, or at least use it prudently. It is enough to stress that it is not in any way a salad for bachelors." This endorses the fact that the content of potassium in celery promotes sexual activity, and the Vitamin A works with the Vitamin E to increase muscular and glandular activity. In Roman times, celery was dedicated to the god of sex, Pluto. In the Middle Ages, it was placed under a pregnant woman's bed in the belief that she would give birth to a boy child. Celery helps in combating ageing in arteries, is good for the muscles, and helps circulation by reducing cholesterol levels in the blood.

CELERIAC
Celeriac is best known for the nutty flavour of its bulbous roots, which are used as a vegetable. This plant also contains an essential oil, which is used to flavour a salt-based seasoning and various sauces. Preparations from the oil are used in treatments for asthma, bronchitis, liver diseases and fevers. A sleep-promoting tea is also made from the Celeriac seeds which contain pig pheromones, an aphrodisiac essential in the mutual attraction of male and female.

ENDIVE

This vegetable is noted for purifying the blood, for its invigorating effects and as an effective tonic. Endives have a long history of being used in love potions and philtres for this reason.

GINSENG

In recent years, the 'man-root' ginseng has come into its own as a stimulant and aphrodisiac. For 5000 years, the strengthening properties of ginseng have been revered in China and the East, where Emperors and poets praised the root and its effects on the libido.

HORSERADISH

The Spanish name for this plant reflects the pungency of its root, Rabano picante, or hot radish. It is the root of this vegetable which is used in cookery, generally grated and mixed with cream to make a sauce. Horseradish contains Vitamin C, and is a good diuretic with antibiotic qualities.

Horseradish has a long history of sexual connotation, mostly for the lengths to which the white root can extend. Some roots have been measured in many metres, and it is a most prolific plant once it takes hold.

IRIS

An aphrodisiac powder is made from 10g of ground iris rhizome, 10g of freshly grated ginger, 10g of ground cinnamon and 150g of honey, infused in a bottle of good white wine. Let this stand overnight, then strain and add 2 tablespoons of milk, 6 freshly ground almonds reduced to a powder, and leave to infuse for a week in a well stoppered bottle. Shake at regular intervals.

MANDRAKE

Very similar to the horseradish, the mandrake (Mandragora officianarum) was held to be one of the most magical of root vegetables, mostly because of the humanoid shape of its root. This root was a well sought after love talisman, and herbalists once set down guidelines on drawing this potent root from the ground. On the night of a full moon, the mandrake hunter would take his pet dog with him. The dog was tied to the mandrake's stalk and its owner retired to a safe distance. The dog was then called by its master, thus drawing the man-shaped root from the ground. The root was then cut from its leaves with a knife fashioned in the shape of a man or woman, and holes cut into the root. Into these holes were placed millet seeds, and the root was buried in the ground until it became covered with hairs. The root was then dug up and used as a potent love charm.

MUSHROOMS AND TRUFFLES

The aphrodisiac qualities of mushrooms have been known since ancient times. Just the musky odour of mushrooms, especially that of the morel, the shiitake and the truffle, is dark and secret and strangely sexy. Many mushrooms and fungi also have an erotic, phallic shape and the truffle's spherical shape and aphrodisiac powers are legendary. Four thousand years ago, the Babylonians were known to have appreciated the properties of the truffle, as did the Athenians, and the great gastronomes of the ancients – Pliny, Apicus and Athenaeus – all wrote in praise of truffles. Apicus favoured recipes with a combination of ceps mushrooms and truffles, and the Emperor Claudius regularly ordered vast quantities of truffles for his Roman orgies. Eventually his wife, Agrippina, poisoned him with a secret mushroom concoction, although it is not known whether the content of lethal fungi was deliberate or a genuine mistake. King Louis XIV, the 'Grand Monarque' of France, was said to have consumed a pound of truffles a day. It was during his reign that the great gastronome, La Varenne, created the celebrated 'duxelles', a mushroom sauce made, it is said, for the Marquis d'Uxelles.

In Louis XV's day, his paramour, Madame de Pompadour, created an aphrodisiac potion consisting of truffles, celery and vanilla. At the same time, Casanova swore by the aphrodisiac effects of black truffles, and Napoleon was also said to order black truffles daily. Honore de Balzac wrote, "If a truffle falls on my plate, it immediately hatches ten new characters for my 'Comedie Humaine'". The French author Colette, and Marcel Boulestan, the gastronomic writer, also dined on "pounds of beautiful truffles, cooked under the ashes." Colette called truffles "the jewels of the poor soil."

Unlike most mushrooms, truffles cannot be artificially cultivated and must be searched for in the wild. In the Perigord region of France, they are known locally as truffes, or 'gout de terrior'. Truffles are an unusual, pungent and expensive delicacy. They are not an attractive fungi. In the raw state, the truffle is a black, or occasionally grey or white knobbly mass, ranging in size from that of a golf ball to the size of a fist. The Perigord black truffle is the most highly prized variety although there are more than 30 types. Truffles are rare and time-consuming to find. Their woody locations are jealously guarded local secrets, and feuds have regularly irrupted over infringement on truffle-rich territories. Hence the truffle hunters, or caveur, walk at night between December and February in search of their elusive quarry.

Trained pigs and dogs, sensitive to the truffle aroma, are used to locate truffles. This is because the truffle emits a pheromone undetectable by humans, but which the male pig gives off to excite the female. Truffles can be found between two centimetres and a metre below the soil, often near the roots of hazel, holm-oak and especially the white oak trees which cover many hillsides in the Dordogne Valley. The oaks under which the best truffles are found are known as 'chenes trufferes'. The main regions for truffle production are Bergerac, Brantone (which holds a 'foire des truffes' annually at Christmas), Coly, Domme, Excideuil, Perigueux, Sarlat, Sorges, Terrasson, Thenon and Thiviers. There is hardly a recipe in the region that cannot be improved with the addition of shavings of the precious truffle. Even scrambled eggs take on a completely new guise when grated truffles are added – they become 'bouillade perigourdine'. In this region, truffles are widely used in culinary preparations from poultry stuffings to casseroles, from foie gras to sausages.

The chemical properties of fungi reveal their aphrodisiac qualities. The average mushroom contains between 70-90% vegetable protein, with a high essential amino acid and folic acid content. Folic acid is a known blood-builder. One hundred grams of mushrooms contains 620mg of potassium and a high pantothenic acid content. Potassium is essential in testosterone production. The Vitamin B12 content in mushrooms is the only vegetable source of this essential vitamin, they are low in fat and cholesterol, and have virtually no calorific content.

ONIONS

All forms of onions (Allium cepa), including scallions, shallots leeks and spring onions are essential ingredients for many dishes worldwide. Medicinally, onions are good for asthma, coughs and colds and have an antiseptic quality. Onions were known in ancient times as the 'Food of the Gods', and Ovid, the Roman poet, recommended eating white shallots with herbs and honey as an aphrodisiac, and for the unrequited lover, a diet devoid of onions.

The ancient Egyptians and Hindus banned their priests from eating onions, as it distracted from their sacred duties, and the ancient Greeks swore by onions as aphrodisiacs. In 'The Perfumed Garden', an Abou el Heloukh was said to have remained in a constant state of sexual stimulation for thirty days through solely eating onions. It does not mention how many onions Abou consumed, or who benefited from this marathon feat! Culpeper suggests that onions "increase sperm, especially the seed, and provoke women's courses." French onion soup has also long been known as an effective aphrodisiac, and was traditionally served at wedding feasts. The recipe included glazing two onions in butter, boiling them in a pint of milk, liquidising them, mixing in an egg and seasoning with salt and pepper.

SOYA

A major ingredient in many sauces, the soya bean has numerous uses. This small, round, yellowish bean has the highest nutritional value of any bean, and contains protein, Vitamin B and low cholesterol unsaturated fats. When the beans are left to sprout they become rich in Vitamin C. Soya is part of the leguminosae family, and is a major crop in the US and in Asia, where soy sauce is produced from the fermentation of cooked soya beans, roasted wheat and salt. This is a brown, tangy sauce, often used as an ingredient in other sauces, and widely used in cooking. Soya flour is made from grinding the beans, and the meal can be used in baking. A cooking oil is also extracted from the soya bean, and the protein is widely used in vegetarian cookery.

SUNFLOWER

Native to the Americas, the seeds of the sunflower (Helianthus annus) are a nutritious food and a useful oil is crushed from them. The plant can grow to 12 foot, and has a large head of seeds surrounded by yellow petals. Their association with the sun led the Aztecs to revere the plant, to which they attributed special powers. The seeds have expectorant qualities and are used in a medicinal diuretic. A form of coffee is made from the dried, ground seeds. The flower buds can be eaten boiled, and the dried leaves were once used as a herbal tobacco. Early herbalists recommended that a potent 'provoker of lust', was sunflower seeds boiled in fat with pepper added.

SWEET POTATO

Sweet potatoes (Ipomoea batatas) or Batatas, a native of the New World, are also widely grown worldwide. The name comes from the Arawak Amerindian word 'batatas', from where the word potato derives. Propagation is achieved through planting a leafy stem, called a slip. A mass of vine grows above ground, as the pointed tuber forms underground. The tuber's smooth skin is either white or a pale reddish colour, and the flesh is usually white or orange. The flesh is mainly starch but contains sugar and some protein. Sweet potato is generally boiled and mashed, and has a chestnut flavour. To cook, they should be peeled and cut into pieces, then brought to the boil. They should then be covered and simmered for 30 to 40 minutes, until soft. In the 16th century, Europeans endowed the sweet potato with aphrodisiac qualities, and even Shakespeare had his Falstaff cry, "Let the sky rain potatoes!" when he planned to seduce the merry wives of Windsor.

TOMATOES

The tomato (Lycopersicon esculentum) is a member of the Solanaceae family, which includes henbane, nightshade, chillies, peppers, aubergine, the potato and tobacco. It is really the fruit of a herbaceous plant, native to South America, discovered by the Spanish during the conquest of Mexico, where it had been used for thousands of years. The tomato is now one of the most common food ingredients. When it was first brought to Europe in the 16th century, the tomato was named the 'pomme d'amour', or 'love apple'. Tomatoes will grow in most climates, and the fruit is generally green when unripe and red when ripe. However, there are numerous varieties of tomato where colour varies, as does the shape. Most tomatoes are glossy-skinned and usually spherical in shape. The Currant and Cherry tomatoes are very small and round, compared to the Beef tomato, which can be 20 times the size of the Cherry. There are also the pear-shaped tomatoes, which are often seen canned and known as Plum or Italian tomatoes. The leaves and stalks of the tomato contain poisonous alkaloids, known as 'solanins', and it is only the fruit which is eaten. Tomatoes have a thin skin, which can be peeled, made easier by blanching in hot water. They also contain many edible but indigestible seeds. Tomatoes are rich in Vitamins A and C, and iron, and are a source of sugar with a high water content. They are readily available in cans, bottled, as pureé, juiced, dried or fresh. They are widely used in sauces, relishes, pickles, chutneys and ketchup, or catsup.

The Perfect Partner

Although there are almost fifty commonly used herbs, spices and aromatic seeds, as well as other ingredients used in sauces, around 20 of these are traditional accompaniments to certain dishes. The following charts are intended as guidelines only.

Herb and Spice Selection Chart

Salads – burnet, chervil, chives, dill, fennel, lovage

Egg dishes – basil, burnet, chervil, chives, dill, fennel, marjoram, parsley, sage

Cheese – basil, caraway, chives, dill, fennel, marjoram, parsley, sage

Soups – basil, bay, caraway, chives, dill, fennel, marjoram, lovage, parsley, sage, tarragon, thyme

Vegetables – basil, bay, caraway, chives, cumin, dill, fennel, lovage, marjoram, oregano, parsley, sage, savory, tarragon, thyme

Fish – bay, chervil, chives, dill, fennel, parsley, savory, sorrel, tarragon

Chicken – basil, bay, chervil, dill, fennel, juniper, marjoram, parsley, sorrel, tarragon, thyme

Duck/Goose – coriander, juniper, marjoram, sage, tarragon

Game – basil, bay, coriander, juniper, lovage, marjoram, parsley, tarragon, thyme

Beef – basil, bay, coriander, lovage, marjoram, oregano, rosemary, sage, tarragon, thyme

Lamb – basil, bay, coriander, dill, fennel, juniper, lovage, marjoram, rosemary, tarragon, thyme

Pork – basil, bay, caraway, coriander, juniper, marjoram, sage, tarragon

Veal – basil, bay, chervil, coriander, marjoram, parsley, tarragon

The Sweet and the Sour

A number of sauce ingredients are used as emulsifiers or to add a tart, sweet or sour flavour to the finished product.

Four products of the sugar cane, as well as sugar itself, are also commonly used in commercial sauces. These are molasses, which is a dark and very sweet sugar syrup. It is formed as a residue when raw sugar is being refined and is also in the manufacture of rum and ethyl alcohol. The second widely used sugar product used in sauces is caramel, which is sugar syrup that has been heated until it turns a light brown colour. The third and fourth sauce sugar products are golden syrup and treacle.

Wines, usually red wine and sherry, are also used in sauces as are various vegetable oils, such as the oil pressed from sunflower seeds. Sherry is a fortified wine that has been made with fermented white grapes to which brandy has been added. Both lemon and lime juice and their oils are ingredients in some sauces and are widely used in marinades, particularly those for fish and seafood. Soya bean extract, soy sauce and wheat flour are also commonly used in many commercial sauces.

Culinary Vinegars

Both spirit vinegar and malt vinegar are common ingredients, imparting their own special flavour. Malt vinegar is the strongest of the two, and is based on beer, and is formed by the action of acetic acid bacteria on the alcohol. The word vinegar comes from the French for sour wine; 'vin' for wine and 'aigre' for sour. Almost any alcoholic liquid can be soured into vinegar as any alcoholic beverage left in contact with air becomes vinegar. The slower the vinegar is matured in its oak casks, the better it is. It was Louis Pasteur who devised the perfect recipe for vinegar in 1867 and today Orleans in France is now the largest centre for vinegar production. Most culinary vinegars are made with cider, white or red wines, although the Japanese produce a sweet vinegar from rice.

Herbs and spices are also used in cooking vinegars, which in turn are often a main ingredient of sauces and marinades. Selected herbs and spices are macerated or steeped in wine vinegar for up to three weeks, letting the flavour and aroma infuse into the vinegar, after which the mixture is pressed and then filtered. There are around 15 main types of vinegar, including garlic, red wine, cider chilli and green pepper vinegars. The basic vinegars are malt and spirit vinegar.

Dill and Fennel vinegar has an infusion of both herbs and is a favourite accompaniment to fish dishes, salads and is used in pickling.

Mint vinegar is used in mint sauce for lamb dishes and also for marinating lamb. It also goes will with salads.

Provencal vinegar is prepared with a combination of aniseed, bay, rosemary, sage, sweet pepper and tarragon. It is excellent for preparing sauces used in stews or as a marinade or seasoning.

Red Basil vinegar can be used to marinade chicken and lamb and for spicy sauces. This aromatic vinegar is also good with salads and pasta dishes.

Spice vinegar is made with an infusion of allspice, cinnamon, cloves and ginger and makes a fine accompaniment to beef casseroles. This spicy, red wine vinegar is also good to braise vegetables with.

Tarragon vinegar is a classic ingredient of sauces such as mayonnaise, hollandaise or bearnaise, and is also used in vinaigrettes for fish, game or chicken dishes.

There was also a concoction supposedly used by grave robbers in the 17th century's great plague which beset Europe, and it was known as the Vinegar of the Four Thieves. It consisted of malt vinegar, cloves, lavender, marjoram and rosemary but was used medicinally rather than as a culinary preparation.

Marinades

All cooks have a variety of favourite marinade recipes, which impart aroma and flavour to meat and fish dishes before cooking and which also help to tenderise the flesh. Marinades, a word of French origin, are seasoned liquids in which fish or meat is left to marinate or soak either for a matter of a few hours or sometimes even for days. The classic marinade is a mixture of wine vinegar, olive oil, lemon or lime juice, chopped onion and garlic, the herb or spice appropriate for the meat or fish and salt and pepper. Some classic marinades might include the following:

For pork use a mixture of marsala, garlic, orange juice and rind, parsley and saffron.

For red meat, try a combination of red wine, brandy olive oil, bay, peppercorns and thyme.

For game, use a marinade of port, chopped onions, fine herbes and redcurrant jelly.

For fish most marinades consist of lime or lemon juice and a selection of herbs such as bay, chives, dill, fennel and tarragon.

Sometimes, sweet marinades are used to infuse a flavour into fruit and these generally consist of a mixture of liqueur and fruit juice.

Index

Books by Andy Gravette

Cuba, An Introduction
Cuba, A Natural History
Official Guide to Cuba
Cuba – Guide
Globetrotter's Guide to Cuba
Map Guide to Cuba
Map Guide to the Canary Islands
The Traveller's Guide – Netherlands Antilles
Explorer Guide to the Caribbean
Globetrotter's Guide to the Canary Islands
Insight Guide to the Eastern Canary Islands
Insight Guide to the Gambia and Senegal
Landmark Guide to the Gambia
The European Hotel Guide
French Hotel Guide
Visitors Guide to Egypt
Visitors Guide to the Balearic Islands
Windrush – Sardinia
Windrush – Madeira
Suntree Guide to Italy
Architectural Heritage to the Caribbean
Slainte! A Taste of Old Ireland
The Story of Rum in the Caribbean
The Story of the Cuban Cigar
Caribbean Barbecue Cookery
Classic Cuban Cookery

Books from Vision

Feng Shui Cookbook
Elizabeth Miles

There is Fire-roasted Fillet Mignon with Wild Mushroom Sauce for those who seek motivation and peak performance. To fight burnout, experience the relaxing yin energy in a serving of cool Gingered Sweet Potato Soup. A delectable slice of Aubergine, Tomato and Chevre Tart brings out one's feminine side for contemplation and learning, while Chilli-Honey Barbecued Baby Back Ribs unleash masculine yang energy for daring endeavours and big challenges. In addition, you might want to try:

Drunken Firepot Shrimp
Tomato Timbales with Avocado and Cream
Hot and Sour Mangoes
Pork and Shrimp Wantons with Coriander Pesto
Warm Scallop Salad with Green Beans and Almonds

Whatever your yin/yang needs, there is a delicious recipe here to satisfy your palate and re-energize your body and mind.

ISBN: 1-901250-34-2
Price: £10.99
Published by Vision Paperbacks

The Erotic Cookbook
Cristina Moles Kaupp

The Romantic 'Diner a Deux' is a ritual as old as time itself, and has always been a prelude to fantastic sex. Eve may have seduced Adam with a mere apple, but The Erotic Cookbook explores the most intimate relationship between desire and fine food.

The ancient secrets of culinary conquest and the effects of aphrodisiacs, past and present are shared, and the ingredients for seduction are incorporated into mouth-watering recipes from all over the world.

Over 90 innovative and easy-to-follow recipes have been designed to tempt readers (and their loved ones) into the realms of sensual bliss.

The Erotic Cookbook includes enticing and saucy dishes, such as Oysters in Champagne Sauce, Geisha Soup, Spicy Smoked Goose Breast with Melon and Fresh Ginger, Papardelle with Black Truffles and wonderful desserts like 'Up All Night' Espresso Mousse.

This is a book for lovers of all ages who are keen on enhancing the pleasure of passion.

ISBN: 1-901250-33-4
Price £6.99
Published by Vision Paperbacks

Classic Cuban Cookery
Andy Gravette

Cuban Cuisine is a melting pot of the culinary traditions of 4 continents. African, South American, North American and European cuisines combine to produce a mouth-watering – and unique – style of cooking.

Recipes include Rainbow Peanut Soup, Cuban Papaya Cheese, Empanadas, Havana Pickle Sauce, Quiqui Marina's Caldosa Stew, Cuban Conch Salad, Trout in Coconut Sauce, Zapote Sorbet and Coconut Cream Pie. There is also a wide range of cocktails, including three varieties of the famous Daiquiri and a host of exotic coffees.

The author, Andy Gravette, has spent 15 years researching and enjoying Cuban food while travelling the country. He prefaces each chapter with a profile of a famous Havana restaurant. He also highlights the history of Cuban ingredients, giving depth to this, the first Classic Cuban Cookbook.

ISBN: 1-901250-39-3
Price: £10.99
Published by Fusion Press

All Vision Paperbacks and Fusion Press titles are available from good bookshops.

You can place an order for our titles with our distributor:
TBS Ltd.
Call their orders hotline on
01206 255637

Fusion Press and Vision Paperbacks
20 Queen Anne Street
London W1M 0AY
Phone: +44 270 323 9757
Fax: +44 270 323 9747
Email: sheenadewan@compuserve.com